I'm Published! Now What?

An author's guide to creating successful
book events, readings, and promotions

by

Jeffrey S. Copeland

PARAGON HOUSE
SAINT PAUL, MINNESOTA

First Edition 2016

Published in the United States by
Paragon House
Saint Paul, Minnesota

www.ParagonHouse.com

Cover Design by Jayna Anderson

Library of Congress Cataloging-in-Publication Data

Copeland, Jeffrey S. (Jeffrey Scott), 1953-
  I'm published! Now what? / Jeffrey S. Copeland.
     pages cm
  Includes bibliographical references.
Summary: "This practical guide to conducting successful book readings,
events, and promotions will help you understand and navigate the shifting
sands of the publishing world. This guide will help demystify book
marketing and prepare authors to work effectively with bookstore event
coordinators, the best friends authors can have inside the stores. Copeland
also shares what to do after events to maximize and build upon success"--
Provided by publisher.

  ISBN 978-1-55778-919-8 (paperback)

  1. Books--Marketing. 2. Authorship--Marketing. I. Title.
  Z285.6.C67 2015
  070.5'2--dc23

                              2015018400

Manufactured in the United States of America

10 9 8 7 6 5 4 3 2 1

The paper used in this publication meets the minimum requirements of
American National Standard for Information Sciences—Permanence of
Paper for Printed Library Materials, ANSIZ39.48-1984.

For all the bookstore event coordinators and authors who shared their expertise and put up with me as I discovered another side of the wonderful world of book events

CONTENTS

INTRODUCTION

> *"A book is a device to ignite the imagination."*
> —Alan Bennett

One of the greatest milestones of a writer's life happens when word comes that a piece long worked on—quite often with blood, sweat, and tears thoroughly mixed together—will be published. It does not matter if the work is published by a mainstream publisher or self-published through one of the many e-publishers/e-retailers. What matters most is the creative effort has found a home and will be "out there" for others to read and enjoy. This day is a culmination of all the background research, composing, revising, editing, and formatting. The pure joy and overwhelming euphoria, the satisfaction of accomplishment (add drum roll and fireworks here) all come together to make the experience one never to be forgotten. However, this period of practically floating on air all too soon gives way as hard reality sets in, most typically in the form of this question:

"I'm published! Now what?"

The "Now what?" that follows is often the most important consideration of all. The "Now what?" is the long road to achieving successful book readings, events, and promotions. These are the life-blood of any new publication, and without these, your hard-earned work can quickly wither and die on the bookshelves, never seen by those who would have read and enjoyed it. Basically, this is the age-old question: "If a tree falls in a forest and no one is around to hear it, does it still make a sound?" That same question, with a few adjustments in wording, applies *directly* to publication of your work: "If a piece is published and no one knows about it, will it be read?" The answer, quite simply, is "No!" Therefore, once a work is published, you must immediately begin this next phase of the publishing process.

For many new writers, this road to achieving successful book readings, events, and promotions can be full of potholes and unexpected twists and turns, not to mention a fair amount of mystery and confusion. And, sadly, the route is most often learned by trial-and-error (with emphasis on *error*). However, this does not have to be the case. While publishing has changed much in recent years and it is often difficult for even veteran writers to keep up with the constant "shifting sands" of the industry, you can have a positive start on this journey by building upon tried-and-true practical advice, advice that will be provided and explained in detail in this book.

The Changing World of Publishing

Just about every author, at some point, has a version of the following dream:

An author makes contact with the owner of a large and popular bookstore. The author's message reads simply: "My travels bring me to your town next week. Would you like me to stop by to do a reading from my new book?"

The bookstore owner is overjoyed and immediately responds in the affirmative. One week later, the author comes to the bookstore, where dozens of book lovers wait, all excited to listen to and interact with a master of words and tales. The bookstore owner, quite pleased by the large turnout, immediately benefits from the community's goodwill and the profits from the sales of the author's book. Representatives of the local media also show up to record the event for those in the surrounding area not fortunate enough to take part. The reading is a tremendous success, and all involved are pleased beyond words.

This is a beautiful dream, one shared by authors and bookstore representatives alike, but today, this dream becomes a reality only when *created* through a tremendous amount of hard work and collaboration by *both* the bookstore representatives and the author. Oh, book readings and events still happen during which dozens of eager book lovers show up, and bookstore owners are still excited by the prospect of hosting writers at their stores. But for this to happen, a perfectly balanced relationship must exist among bookstores, authors, and publishers.

Long gone are the days when book readings could be scheduled at a moment's notice. Gone are the days when large audiences appeared "just to hear an author read"—when it was still something of a novelty to rub elbows with those who put words to page. Gone are the days when bookstores and libraries were the only places one could find an author's book(s). Today, nearly everything—from what authors and booksellers do to get ready for book events to how and where books are touted and sold—rolls with the shifting sands of the publishing world.

This book—this practical guide to conducting successful book readings, events, and promotions—will help you understand and navigate these shifting sands. It will pull back the curtain to help demystify just how you can build successful readings, events, and promotions. Through this guide, you will learn how to prepare for these areas and how to work effectively with bookstore event coordinators, the best friends authors can have inside the stores.

Recent Trends and Developments

More than ever before, you must have knowledge of recent trends and developments in publishing. These have dramatically changed, either directly or indirectly, how book readings, events, and promotions take place.

Not long ago, with any type of persistence and self-promotion, a new or established author could wrangle book events at bookstores. Now, however, each month more "brick-and-mortar" bookstores close. We've already seen the demise of Borders, Waldenbooks, and a host of independent bookstores—and others are struggling. These closings have dramatically reduced potential venues for readings and events, making this part of the publishing/selling world much more difficult for an author to enter. Those stores left standing are reluctant to host book readings and events because the outlay of work and expense to put them on properly doesn't always match the return on such investment. In short, many bookstores build significant goodwill with their customers—but lose a great deal of money—by having authors to their stores.

At the same time, e-book publications and e-readers have proliferated and are, according to many, partly to blame for the closing of so many brick-and-mortar stores. In recent years e-book sales have equaled or surpassed traditional hardback book sales, a trend that will, no doubt, continue to grow. While this has not been good for most of the traditional bookstores, authors now have many more options for publication of their work through e-publishers/retailers. However, this trend is both a blessing and a curse. If traditional bookstores continue to close at the current rate, many in publishing fear we could end up with just one or two "retail giants" controlling book sales. If that happens, the world of publishing/bookselling as we know it will be forever changed—and how authors work and how their books are promoted will be transformed right along with it.

How readers browse titles is likewise changing dramatically. As more readers turn to e-devices, they find out about books and receive recommendations for books through these same e-devices: Amazon Kindle Library, Barnes & Noble Nook Library, Apple i-Store Library, and so forth. Dozens of online book review sites now exist as well—such as Goodreads.com, BookReporter.com, AllReaders.com, BookPage.com—and all of these direct readers toward authors and books. Even many of our public libraries are going digital, which further influences what people read and how readers find and interact with books. Along with this, more authors create a "digital persona" and/or "digital footprint" through the use of author blogs, websites, and social media (Snapchat, Instagram, Tumblr, Reddit, Vine, LinkedIn, Pinterest, and others) to bring readers and books together by way of the Internet. This e-revolution in publishing has for better or worse directly changed book readings, events, and promotions.

Until recently, book readings and events were almost exclusively the province of writers published through the mainstream publishing houses and, at times, a number of dedicated self-published authors who tended to remain in their local areas. At the traditional brick-and-mortar bookstores, authors typically read short portions of their work and then answered a few questions from those assembled. The perception was that authors were a small and exclusive club, and readers came to meet and rub shoulders with "literary celebrities." These events augmented advertising done by publishing houses, and were a major way of finding out about books and authors.

In recent years these events have moved more toward "edutainment" and "performance art." Because so much information about a given book is already on the Internet before an author shows up for an event, those in the audience have come to expect more than just a traditional reading. Today, authors often offer information about the type of writing being shared, explain how the particular work came about, provide a glimpse into the process of writing, let all know where and how the work can be purchased (the full range of venues and versions)—and do all of this while entertaining the readers. Authors are now, more than ever, expected to be self-promoters and publicists.

Another part of the publishing landscape that has changed greatly is that authors are no longer a "small and exclusive club." In fact, it seems everyone is writing a book. For example, at a recent workshop I conducted, thirty-eight of the forty-five present were completing books, mainly poetry, novels, essay collections, or short stories. I asked how many had published books before. Only one had a previous publication. I asked how many currently had contracts with publishers for the work they were creating. At that point, none had contracts. To my surprise, of those in the room, half were seeking publication through mainstream publishers. The other half were preparing for e-publication through Amazon, Barnes & Noble, various Apple venues, KOBO, or other online publishers.

The bottom line for all of this is quite clear: the ranks of authors will continue to grow. Still, *how well* all will prosper depends, in large measure, upon how successful they are in building book readings, events, and promotions. Again, if a tree falls in a forest....

The Road Ahead

It is gross understatement to say the worlds of publishing and bookselling are rapidly changing. Authors must use the best, current knowledge and practices at their readings and events to keep from falling below the shifting sands swirling around them. For new authors in particular, building success right from the beginning is a MUST. To help you prepare for these successes, the information is this guide will be structured as follows:

Section 1:   What you can do in preparation BEFORE conducting book readings, events, and promotions to achieve success.

Section 2:   What you can do DURING book readings, events, and promotions to achieve success.

Section 3:   What you can do AFTER book readings, events, and promotions (and *all the time*) to help maximize and build upon success.

Section 4:   Voices from the road: Authors' suggestions for building successful book events.

Section 5:   And now a word from our sponsors: advice and wisdom from bookstore event coordinators

Section 6:   Appendices: Checklists for authors.

Section 7:   Photos

Section 8:   Contributors.

The results of the "Writer's Dream" mentioned earlier *can* still be achieved. However, achieving that dream takes a considerable amount of knowledge and work. This guide offers practical advice and suggestions to make this dream a reality for those new to the world of publishing—a world of great joy for new authors and established authors as well. I welcome you to this world—and wish you the very best as you begin your journey.

SECTION I

Basic Preparation Before Conducting Readings, Events, and Promotions (Building success before hitting the road!)

> *"You can't wait for inspiration. You have to go after it with a club."*
>
> —Jack London

The success, or failure, of most book events is determined *before* an author gets in front of an audience. The advance *preparation* will most often determine how the events will play out. Think of this analogy: Before leaving for vacation, many people like to study the place where they will be going. Many map out routes. Others make reservations at hotels. Still others check out and make arrangements for side trips once there. Some go as far as preparing a detailed schedule for the vacation so that nothing will be left out during the trip. Such preparation often determines whether the experience will be all it was hoped to be.

In book events and promotions, this degree of preparation is vital to many areas, ranging from coming across as a polished professional to meeting an audience's expectations. This advance work allows you to be prepared for almost any audience or venue, which is critically important considering the variety of experiences—expected and unexpected—that you can encounter while promoting your book. In building a platform for this success, you should consider these six *before* areas.

I. Choosing Appropriate Venues and Audiences

Deciding the proper location and audience for a book event is vital to the event's success. Bookstores are, of course, the first and most logical venue (and they will be covered in detail in the next section), but there are so many other factors to consider. Before deciding upon potential venues for book events, you should answer two questions:

❖ "What are the main areas of content and subject matter explored in my book?"

❖ "Which groups would most like to hear about these areas?"

Answering the first question—"What are the main areas of content and subject matter explored in my book?"—allows you to target potential audiences and venues. This should not be a tough question for you to answer in a brief list. For example, the main subjects and areas explored in my book *Inman's War* are as follows:

> Special military units that served during WWII

> U.S. military history

> History of the "Segregated Battalions" that served in WWII

> St. Louis history (where many of the early events of the book take place)

> Issues of "race" in American history

> Forgotten heroes in American history

Once a list has been composed and evaluated, the logical follow-up question is this: "Which groups would most like to hear about these areas?" For most authors, family and friends are at the top of that list, but a book won't go very far if the list stops there. You should next think of special interest groups who might be interested in the book's subject matter.

I'll again draw upon personal experiences with my book *Inman's War* to provide a few examples. *Inman's War* is about members of a "colored battalion" who served during World War II. After thinking about the main subjects explored in the book, I decided to contact different military groups because I felt they might be interested in hearing about the book and the background research I did in order to write it. I contacted representatives of all branches of the U.S. Armed Services, ROTC groups at schools, a wide variety of veterans groups, and museums and archives with special exhibits and interest in military history. I was pleased to find out dozens of those groups were, indeed, interested in hearing me speak about the book, and I immediately set up a schedule for those events.

At the same time, I felt strongly that groups other than those tied directly to the military would also be interested. After studying the list of subject matter and content of the book again, I contacted a variety of groups/organizations in St. Louis, Missouri, where a significant part of the story takes place. St. Louis has a number of groups devoted to preserving the history of the city—from civic groups to government groups—and many of those were also interested in having me speak about the book. Before long, I had a full schedule of events ahead of me, a wonderful circumstance for a writer.

Along with deciding which groups to target for book events, you should also come up with a list of venues where interested readers might be. The "where" to conduct book events actually has two separate and distinct categories: "local" and "at distance" venues. First think of all the places in your hometown and immediate geographical area where events might be possible. Communities generally love to hear about, and also take pride in, work done by local writers, so there are usually multiple possibilities where events can take place.

Bookstores are, naturally, a good place to begin. This list should include all "chain" retailers, independent booksellers, and university bookstores. You should also think of all other places where books are sold locally. In my town, several restaurants and museums also sell books by local authors, and it doesn't take much more than a visit to these locations and a discussion with the managers/directors to establish both book events and sales of the books there. This also generates more publicity for the work. Local museums are particularly good places to explore because they are always looking for programs and speakers. Schools—both university and public/private schools—are often venues for book events. Most communities also have writer groups and clubs, and they, too, are always on the watch for speakers. Again, the list of "subject matter and content" within a book should be matched to the types of groups and organizations that exist in and around the surrounding area.

"At distance" events are just as important, but are somewhat more difficult to arrange, mostly because of travel issues. Still, an author should consider the places across the country, and around the globe, for that matter, where book events could take place. For example, while getting their training before going overseas, the soldiers in *Inman's War* spent time in several other towns across the country. These ranged from towns in Arizona to Texas to Tennessee to Virginia. I contacted representatives of civic groups and organizations in those towns to see if they might be interested in hearing more about their history. Many of them did, which added even more stops on my growing list of upcoming events. For my other books, I've traveled to do events all across the United States—and everywhere from the United Kingdom to Europe to Central America.

However, when scheduling "at distance" events, you should always weigh the potential benefits and potential drawbacks of making the travel. Will the event help promote the book in a special way? Will the audience(s) there be sufficient to justify the expense of the travel? Carefully consider these and other questions like them, before scheduling "at distance" events.

When the drawbacks of traveling are too great, another option to consider is using the new technologies that are coming out by the day. For instance, I recently used "FaceTime," via my cell phone, to communicate with multiple groups at the same time. I was attending a professional conference in New Orleans, Louisiana, on a day when several groups from the Midwest had asked if I could come visit with them about one of my books. It was impossible to meet with them in person, as I was well over a thousand miles away. However, by linking to the readers through FaceTime (by way of my cell phone on my end—and through FaceTime via computers on the other end), we were all able to see and interact with each other quite effectively. I presented information about my book, and the audience was able to ask questions and make comments. And all of this was done while I was seated on a bench just outside St. Louis Cathedral, at Jackson Square, a most wonderful setting for conducting the session—and a location with an important connection to the story we were discussing. A final note: through FaceTime, I was also able to use my cell phone to "show" those with whom I was visiting the surroundings there at Jackson Square and bring New Orleans "live" to them, which all very much appreciated.

It should be noted, however, that FaceTime is just one vehicle that can be used for "distance" presentations when you can't meet with groups—or when you deem it a more efficient use of time for everyone involved. This technology, and the others like it (Skype, for example, is another popular platform), are constantly evolving, and you should do everything possible to keep up with the changes. Doing so opens up whole new worlds of opportunities—for both authors and readers.

II. Getting Invited to the Bookstore: Self-Promotion 101

While this section is specifically geared to working with bookstores, the same activities and principles apply to contacting and working with other groups.

Unless a book has incredible advance sales or the author is very well known (and many times not even then!), bookstores are not going to contact an author to do a book event. Bringing an author to a bookstore is seldom a financial windfall for the store because the time spent in promotion and the number of "people-hours" required to get an event ready can negate any profits from sales of the book.

Why, then, do bookstores continue to have authors stop by to visit with their customers? Most often the answer is that book events are one way of bringing people into the store who might otherwise not come in to browse around and see everything the store has to offer; in short, book events showcase the *bookstore* as much as the author/book being presented. The publicity from book events also reminds regular customers that it might be time to stop in again and see what the store has in the way of new offerings and services. Book events are definitely a two-way street. Authors present their new books, and bookstores take the opportunity to show themselves off to new and old patrons alike.

Given that most bookstores are not going to contact you to come do events, how, then, do you get yourself into the stores? The answer to this question is this: self-promotion. You *must* take the initiative by contacting the bookstores directly and inquiring about the possibility of doing an event. I recommend this process for making that contact.

First, send a short query letter or email to the Event Coordinator of a store.

You can call the bookstore before writing the letter to get the event coordinator's name so the note can be personalized. Such a query letter should have the following parts:

➢ Express your interest in doing a book event at the store;

➢ Be specific about which type of event you'd like to do (a reading, signing, special presentation, a combination of these, and so forth);

➢ Explain why you feel an event would be beneficial to the store and/or the local community;

➢ Politely ask the event coordinator to contact you to discuss the possibility of doing the event—and

express your willingness to do all possible on your
end to help build the success of the event.

➤ Provide your full contact information, everything
from phone numbers to mailing address(es) to
electronic contact information.

A template/sample for building this query letter is
located in *Appendix A.*

If a response to the query letter does not arrive
within a few weeks, I recommend a follow-up phone call
to the event coordinator. During this phone call, you can
remind the event coordinator of the earlier correspon-
dence as a way to break the ice and move to a conversation about doing an event at the store.

This method will not always result in an invitation
for you to come to the store. However, it will let the bookstore know you and your book are out there, and the
Event Coordinator might have suggestions about other
venues/groups in the area that you might approach.

Information about bookstores in the local and
surrounding areas will be easy to obtain. However, you
may also want to contact stores in other places in the
United States or abroad. A simple Internet search with
the words "Best Independent Bookstores" will result in
dozens of lists, which can then be used to contact the
Event Coordinators at targeted locations.

III. Creating Presentations for Events

One of the most important decisions you can make before going out to do book events is what type of pre-sentation will get audiences excited about the book. This can also be an area of great anxiety because most authors don't have backgrounds as professional speak-ers, and the thought of getting in front of an audience fills them with dread. However, whether you are a vet-eran of speaking to groups or a novice, it is *not* difficult to build successful presentations. Basically, there are two main types of presentations.

The "Traditional" Book Event (low-tech)

The traditional book event follows a predictable pattern: an author speaks briefly about herself/himself and the work, reads a short passage or two, and then responds to questions from the audience. This type of presentation is common because, quite frankly, most new authors don't know what else to do when talking about a new book. There is absolutely nothing wrong with choos-ing to do this traditional approach, and there are some practical guidelines to follow to make sure the event is a success.

This traditional presentation is similar to a "lesson plan" created by teachers. A lesson plan is a *guide* teach-ers follow while presenting information to their students that helps keep the teachers focused and on track—and helps them achieve their goals and objectives. You can benefit from the same sort of guide, one that will allow you to build the best possible presentation for your audiences. A traditional book presentation has these features:

A. Introduction

❖ Begin by thanking the host of the event (the bookstore or other group) for having you there to speak about your book—and let everyone know how happy/excited you are to be with them.

❖ Even if you have already been introduced, take a few moments to share something else about yourself, especially if you have *any* type of tie to the town or a special group in attendance. Or, if it is your first time at the venue, say something positive about the store, the group in attendance, or the local community. In other words, build the initial rapport and common bond with your audience.

> NOTE: Some authors like to put the audience at ease and prepare the mood for the talk by telling a short, humorous anecdote related to the book. Some authors can pull this off; others cannot. There is a risk that what one person finds funny or entertaining another will find offensive. Tread cautiously when attempting to include the humorous beginning.

B. Background

❖ Tell how your book came about and how it was

written. This does not have to be long, but give your audience some information about why you chose to write this book—and, if possible, some of your adventures along the way to getting it published.

C. The Reading

- ❖ Choose one or two passages that will spark interest in the book.

- ❖ Do *not* give away the whole story. If you do that, why would those in the audience want to purchase the book?

- ❖ Each passage should be an "exciter" or a "teaser" that makes audience members so interested in the book they will soon be standing in line to purchase it and have you autograph it for them.

D. Q&A

- ❖ Invite questions from the audience. Q&A sessions can be one of the most enjoyable parts of a book event.

E. Conclusion

- ❖ Conclude the presentation by again thanking the appropriate individuals for inviting you to speak about your book.

- ❖ Let the audience know you will be happy to stay for additional questions—and you will be available to autograph books for them after they are purchased.

❖ Ask the person(s) in charge of the event whether
   there are any other announcements that need to be
   made to the crowd. Often, representatives of the
   bookstores will want a few minutes to tell those in
   the audience about other upcoming events. Those
   in charge of organizations or other groups might
   want to share information about upcoming meetings. While these announcements seldom have
   anything to do with you or your book, those in
   charge of the event will appreciate the opportunity
   to share their information.

The Multi-Media Book Event (high-tech)

The traditional format is a fine approach for some, but
many like myself recommend something quite different in both structure and philosophy. Book events are
becoming more "edutainment" and "performance art."
The audience comes not only to hear about the author
and the work but also expects to be entertained. This
has always been the case, but the degree to which the
emphasis has shifted to the "entertainment" side of the
spectrum has increased dramatically. Visuals help provide that entertainment.

   There are several other advantages of using a visual
presentation. First, with the ever-increasing infusion
of technology into our daily lives, people are more
"visual" in how they access and process information. A
visual presentation will most likely match the "knowledge acquisition" style of most of your audience. Plus,

pictures related to the book will add a valuable emphasis and "punch" to the information you present; nothing punctuates a point like a strong visual image. Perhaps the most important reason to use the visual presentation is that it will balance the audience's focus between you and the material being shown. Particularly if you are anxious about standing in front of an audience, placing focus upon "pictures/visuals" can put you more at ease during the event.

The visual presentation provides an additional safety net for authors just getting used to performing before crowds. The pictures and the words that accompany them, and the order in which they are shown, provide a guide or roadmap for the presentation itself. You are still there to present the information, but it is laid out before you through the visuals. Therefore, you do not have to worry about losing your place in the presentation or running off the track. At the same time, the images and accompanying words remind you what should be said at each point in the presentation.

For those just starting out, and even for veteran authors who would like to add this type of presentation, there is a tried-and-true presentation outline that can be used to create the visual presentation. Of course, keep in mind this template might need to be adjusted to fit the specific type of book you have written, but the overall structure and arrangement of the visuals remains basically the same. Think of the presentation as a "slide show"—a visual journey through the material you wish to present to the audience.

In order to create this type of presentation, you should have access to following:

> the Internet (for acquiring free Public Domain images that might be useful for the presentation),

> a good quality scanner (for turning "paper" images into electronic images),

> an electronic device with the capability to take high-resolution photographs (for when you wish to take your own pictures for the presentation).

> an excellent visual presentation program (Many authors favor Microsoft PowerPoint, but other visual presentation formats will work as well.)

With these items available, you are ready to create the presentation. The "slides" in the presentation are as follows—and are listed in an order popular with many authors; however, feel free to adjust the order to suit your particular goals and objectives for the presentation.

Multi-Media Presentation Outline

Title Slide:

A high-resolution photo of the front cover of the book. Because the title of the book is often difficult to read on a photograph of the front cover, the title of the book should also be listed elsewhere on the slide—and be large enough for audiences in the back of the room to be able to read. This is an important beginning to the presentation because this slide will most often be displayed while the audience gathers, while final preparations are made, and even during your introduction. This slide will help set the event's tone.

Author Background Slide(s):

A slide (or two) about YOU. Many authors do not like talking about themselves, but study after study has shown that the "biography of the author" is consistently near the top of the most important areas audiences wish to hear about during book events. Remember, you are selling yourself just as much as the book. You do not have to go into incredible detail—and actually shouldn't—about your life, but audiences have come to expect at least some information about the hobbies and activities authors enjoy when they are not writing. This information can help achieve a nice bond between you and the audience. This slide could show you engaged in activities—or it could be more "generic" and show representative images of the hobbies and activities you enjoy. How personal this becomes is entirely up to you. What is most important here is letting the audience know there is another side to you other than putting words to paper.

If you don't care to share the personal information, a good alternative is to show pictures of and talk about "where" and "how" you write. This involves including images of places where you typically write: your writing area or study in the home, a favorite library or archive, or any other location important to the writing process. In terms of the "how" of writing, you can also share images of rough drafts, storyboards, computer equipment used, and so forth. For some, this information is quite personal and not to be shared; for others, allowing the audience a glimpse into the creative process can lead to great discussion later in the presentation.

Book Background Slide(s):

A slide (or multiple slides) related to how the book came about. Audiences are fascinated by *why* the author chose to write the book. The "story behind the story" is often a wonderful tale that authors can easily share. This slide (or slides) could have images of locations you visited while writing, pictures of those who inspired you or provided information while the book was in progress, or even images of drafts and research materials used. This background information is doubly important because it shows not only how the book came to be, but it also provides additional information about you, which helps create even more of a bond with the audience.

Overview of Book's Subject Slide(s):

This section of the presentation is typically several slides, each with visuals representing something specific about the book's subject matter or specific sections within the work. Show these slides *while* you provide more background about the story. The idea here is to have a visual image to go along with the information being shared verbally.

"First Reading" Slide:

Once the information about the book is presented, the next slide will have a title similar to this: "First Reading"—followed by the page number(s) in the book so those in the audience who already have copies can follow along if they wish. On this slide, try to have a visual image that relates to the content of the specific passage you have chosen to read.

"Second Reading" Slide:

As with the previous slide, include the page number(s) of the second passage you will read aloud. Again, appropriate visual images are included here.

Note: If shorter or additional passages are read, the same format and visual images follow.

"Questions?" Slide:

Once the material in the presentation has been covered, allow members of the audience time to ask questions. A slide with "**Questions?**" in bold typeface, and with any other images you would like to include, is your invitation to those in attendance.

Few people in audiences like to ask the first question, so there will be times when it appears no questions will be forthcoming. An old "author trick" if this happens is to bring to the presentation a couple of questions you have prepared in advance about aspects of the book you really do like to talk about. Write these questions on file cards or print them out on small sheets of paper. Give these to people in the crowd and ask them to pose the questions. Audiences usually find this quite amusing, and responding to the prepared questions usually breaks the ice so that others follow.

If traveling to another country for a book event, where English is not the most common language, consider preparing a special presentation using the native language. Not everything in the presentation needs to be in the other language. Consider adding titles and short summaries to slides. Doing this will greatly help those in the audience who speak English but might still be having a difficult time understanding all that is going on.

I recall one book presentation I did in Costa Rica. While many in the country speak English, I knew others at the event might struggle to grasp some of what would be heard and discussed. Before the trip I prepared all of the major information on the slides in Spanish. After my presentation, many people come up to me and thanked me for doing this. Nearly all of them said they had never had anyone from another country do this before for them, and they were most grateful. Adding another language to a presentation takes a great deal of time. If you can't do this yourself, chances are very good you will know someone who can. Taking this step to show respect for the individuals who come to your presentation will pay strong dividends—and help all reach full enjoyment and understanding.

....

The ultimate goal of the visual presentation is to provide a roadmap and talking points for the time with the audience. Plus, the images themselves add richness to the discussion that can help make the time with the audience exciting and memorable. Creating a visual presentation does take considerable time and effort, but once all is in place, the worthwhile reward for this work will be focused and entertaining events. You should at least experiment with this type of presentation to learn if it matches your individual style of interacting with groups.

Be Prepared

You should actually prepare both types of presentations before meeting with audiences, and there are several reasons this is wise. I've had it happen to me, and I've seen it happen to other authors—a well-planned, high-tech presentation cannot be done because of some problem with either the equipment or because of a sudden change in venue for the event that did not lend itself to the original plan for the presentation. In those cases, an easy switch to a low-tech approach is essential.

I was once scheduled to do my presentation in a large meeting hall, only to find out when I arrived that pipes in the ceiling had burst during the night and the room was flooded. The chairperson of the organization had found a small room in the building next door that was available. That new space was so small many in the audience did not have chairs. The room was also not appropriate for the high-tech presentation I had planned to give. So, I switched quickly to the low-tech presentation, and the event turned out to be one of the best of that whole book tour.

On the other side, I have had events where I originally planned on doing a more informal, low-tech presentation but discovered after getting to the venue that I needed to switch to my other presentation because, much to my surprise, most in the audience had already heard me talk about the book and were coming back for more!

Always plan for the unexpected to take place. If you are prepared for both types of presentations, even if sudden changes happen at the last minute, you can still meet the original goals and objectives with great success.

IV. Gathering Essential Equipment

After conducting hundreds of book events in just about every type of venue and visiting with other authors about their own experiences, I've built a list of equipment you should consider taking along to book events. Some fall into the common sense category, but others on the list may not be that obvious. And keep in mind, the list can be modified and customized. Based upon personal experience and presentation style, you will eventually want to tailor your own "must bring" list of equipment items. However, as you begin, I recommend you bring the following to book events.

Signing Pens

This may seem like a common-sense item, but there are some important considerations here. Unless the theme or subject matter of your book screams for a different color (a friend of mine writes murder mysteries and always signs his books with "blood red" ink), black ink should be used for autographs and inscriptions for a couple of reasons. Publishers typically use black ink for the "front matter" at the beginning of the book, so the black ink of the pen will blend in well with that and help make the signed page more attractive. Black ink also appears more bold and distinct on the page, which purchasers of the book will appreciate. It is not wrong to use other colors, but you should remember the "visual appearance" of the signed page is often just as important to the purchaser of the book as what you write there. A nicely signed page is truly *object de art,* and a keepsake readers will treasure. It is your responsibility to help make that so.

At the same time, there are pens—and then there are pens. It is best to use those with acid-free ink because it will not fade, smear, or "bleed" on the page, which will also help preserve what you have written. I also recommend pens with medium point, "roller bearing" tips. These glide across the page easily, speeding up the time it takes to sign autographs and inscriptions. A roller-bearing pen also takes pressure off the wrist because not as much force is needed when pressing the pen to the page, preventing hand fatigue when you sign large numbers of books.

Do not be cheap when buying signing pens. Most stationary stores will allow authors to try out a full range of pens sold there, so I recommend you try out as many as possible for "feel and fit" before purchase. This may seem way too much effort to put behind selecting a writing utensil, but the reasons behind the effort here will become more clear the first time you experience hand cramping while doing a book signing—and then look up and see a long line of those still waiting for signatures and inscriptions.

Business Cards

Often there will be someone in the audience at a book event who represents a group or organization that would also like to have you come to one of their gatherings to speak about your work. This is one of the many benefits to doing the book events: securing other opportunities to promote your book. When these individuals approach you, be ready to share your contact information quickly. The most efficient way to do this is with specially designed business cards you can hand out. These business cards do not have to be incredibly fancy or striking. Many authors simply type the information and print it out on standard copy paper. Whether professionally printed as regular business cards or simply printed out from a home computer, the contact information should include, at a minimum, the following:

➢ Your full name

➢ Contact information—most typically the e-mail address(es) and/or a business mailing address (in many cases, the address of your publisher)

- ✧ It is generally not wise to include your home address and/or telephone number for the obvious privacy and security reasons.

- ✧ E-mail responses are favored because these can be read *while* you are away conducting book readings and events, which will allow for quicker response to the communication.

- ➢ A list of the groups you are available to address, such as schools, businesses, book clubs, professional organizations, libraries, and so forth

You may also wish to include some of these variations:

- ➢ Visuals such as pictures of book covers or images related to the theme or content of one or more of your books

- ➢ A picture of yourself—to add a personal touch

- ➢ Specific colors and sizes for the cards

  - ✧ Postcard-size contact information seems to be growing in popularity, especially with those who include images with the contact information.

Bookmarks

Bookmarks are very useful for promoting books. First, those who purchase books love bookmarks, especially if they are related to the book they are reading. Some readers even have collections of them. Second, while at a book event, some in the audience might not have time to stay around to purchase the book or may have forgotten to bring their money. A bookmark will allow them to take the book information home with them and, hopefully, purchase the book later on. Bookmarks can also be great conversation starters while you are signing books. There is usually a pretty interesting story behind how the bookmarks were created and why the particular parts of the book were used. Often, that interaction between author and potential reader is enough to sell the book. Finally, some may not wish to purchase the book at that time but would still like your autograph. From my experience, autographed bookmarks are a true treasure for many readers.

An effective bookmark will have at least the following parts/features:

➢ The full title of the book

➢ Your name as it appears on the book

➢ An image or two related to the main subject or theme of the book—to draw the attention of potential readers and build interest in browsing the book

➢ An image of the front cover of the book

➢ A short "teaser" summary of the book, again to build interest in the book

➢ Places where the book can be purchased

Preparing a bookmark for a book is not a difficult task at all. Listed in *Appendix C* are examples of several bookmarks that were used to help promote books. Feel free to use these as models for your own.

I also recommend that you start collecting book-marks, which are generally free and in abundant sup-ply on the counters of bookstores. Looking at the wide range of styles and designs will help you create book-marks appropriate for your own books.

Water, Water, Everywhere!

An author's voice is the most important "piece of equip-ment" at a book event, so great care must be taken to protect it. Regular speaking engagements can often lead to what authors call "dry throat" or "speaker's voice," conditions that make it extremely difficult to communicate with the audience. Keeping hydrated while speaking is one of the easiest methods to com-bat voice problems. Do not assume those in charge of an event will always remember to offer you water. Well over half of those in charge of book events I've done did not offer water; most just simply forgot to ask or didn't think of offering it. Therefore, it is a wise precaution to bring bottled water or some type of water carrier to the event.

In the event sipping water while speaking does not prevent hoarseness or throat irritation, there are a variety of throat lozenges available that will help with the situation. Consult your doctor and/or pharmacist. Many authors also discretely chew gum while speaking because many types of gum help produce saliva, which, in turn, lubricates the throat. You will have to decide upon the best way to protect your voice. What works for one author may not work for another. Still, most would agree that it is best to avoid sugary drinks and candies while speaking because they can actually dry out the throat. In the end, remember to bring water with you; water can protect and save your voice!

A Copy of Your Book with Clearly Marked Passages for Reading Aloud

There is an art and a science to choosing just the right passages to read aloud to audiences during a book event. Many recommend not reading more than two passages without a *very good reason* for adding more. From my own experiences and from watching other authors do readings, I have noticed the audience's attention withers after a couple of passages. Choose sections that best represent what the work is like, either in terms of theme, structure, or content. At the same time, these sections should "tease" the audience and build their curiosity to the point they wish to purchase the book. These passages should also be those which you feel passionate about and enjoy sharing with others. Your enthusiasm for the words will be unmistakable to those in the crowd.

To choose these passages, answer this question: "Which passages in the book would most persuade me to purchase the book?" In other words, which of the sections are most interesting, dramatic, and representative? In choosing which passages to read aloud, I often ask other authors or trusted friends which passages in the book were most interesting to them. Once I know that, I have a good place to start in whittling down the possibilities.

Once you have chosen the passages, you have three tasks:

➢ Clearly mark the passages to be read—both where to begin and where to end. Underline or highlight these so they will be easy to find and follow during the reading.

➢ Practice, practice, practice reading the sections aloud. Nothing ruins a book event more than the author stumbling and fumbling over the words he/she has written.

➢ Time yourself reading these passages while you are practicing them. Often what appears to be a very short section in a book can drag on and on, especially if dialogue is involved. A good, general rule of thumb here is that each passage should be no more than four to five minutes in length. During a reading, that is a long enough time—both for you and your audience.

⬦ Some authors prefer to read several very short passages and talk about them, rather than choosing a couple of longer ones. Practice both with audiences to learn which approach works best with a specific work.

Finally, it is wise to use a very large, bold marker to write your name on the front cover and spine of the copy of the book you will be reading from during the event. I finally started doing this after my own personal copies of many of my books started disappearing at book events.

Note Cards and/or Printed Copy
of the Presentation

Whether you are presenting the more traditional format for a book event or one that will rely heavily on visual presentation, it is always a good idea to have available a "printed guide" detailing what will be shared. Few authors can just fly by the seat of their pants when addressing an audience. Most need "prompts." If you are following the more traditional approach, jot down a few key words or notes on file cards, numbered so that the order is obvious to help keep you on track. The emphasis here is on a "few key words." Do not fill the cards with so much information that what is most important is lost in a mass of words. A few special words and/or phrases on the cards will be most effective and will allow you to keep organized and at pace during the event.

If using a more visual approach, such as PowerPoint, bring along a printed copy of the slides. With the visual presentation printed out, you can easily jot down below the images a few key words to remind you of what to say with each slide. Again, the emphasis here should be on just a *few* words and/or phrases—just enough to keep you moving ahead with the intended plan for the event.

A Good Quality Digital Camera

A wise investment for all authors, a good digital camera is invaluable to have at book events. Photographs taken while at the event are important for refreshing your blogs and websites—and keeping readers up-to-date with your activities and accomplishments. Photos of events can also be used in future promotional materials.

Many cell phones, tablets, and other electronic devices are also capable of taking high-resolution pictures that can be used for a multitude of purposes. However, keep in mind that the high-resolution .jpg format is required for most situations, so take this into consideration when choosing which type of camera to use.

Equipment Essentials for Multi-Media Events

♦ Laptop (and power cord)

The first essential item is a laptop, a tablet, or other device capable of housing a flash drive and/or CD and accessing the Internet. Whether you prefer a Macintosh or PC platform isn't as important as these capabilities. No matter the platform you choose, the visual and audio components in a presentation must be deliverable by *both* Macintosh and PC equipment. In other words, use a neutral program, like Microsoft Office or the equivalent, when preparing materials to share with audiences.

This is important for a very practical reason. Unless you bring your own equipment to an event, you will be at the mercy of whatever system is available at the store.

If you prepare material in a "Macintosh specific" form and then discover that all machines at the bookstore are PC-based and do not have a neutral program/system, your material will be useless. The same would hold true if your material is in a "PC-specific" format and the store is Macintosh-oriented.

In my early days of doing book events, I experienced enough Macintosh/PC compatibility problems at bookstores and other venues that I eventually decided to bring my own equipment so I would always be prepared no matter how the locations were oriented. I've never regretted the decision to acquire my own equipment because this is now one less area of concern when planning events.

Also, remember to always bring your own power cord for the device(s). Most batteries in electronic devices drain quickly, so having a power cord with you will help make sure the equipment always has enough power for the presentation.

♦ Projector

If you wish to augment book events with visual components, you will need a computer projector. The main considerations here are two. First, the projector *must* be compatible with the laptop or other electronic device(s) you will be using. Therefore, do some careful checking to make sure of the equipment compatibility before purchasing a projector. Second, the most important distinction among computer projectors used for author events has to do with the "quality of lumens" within them. "Lumens" refers to the visual quality—brightness, crispness, sharpness of images—of the device. Before purchase, visit with an expert at a retailer that sells computer projectors and explain the type of presentations you intend to do, and ask for appropriate recommendations. A good, general-purpose, middle-cost machine will usually serve just fine.

◆ Extension Cords

Imagine you have brought your own electronic equipment to a book event. The representative of the bookstore or other group has prepared a table where the laptop and projector can be set up for the presentation. Then, after getting the equipment ready, you discover the nearest power outlet is on wall twenty-five feet away—and the power cords on the laptop and projector are only six feet long.

This scenario, unfortunately, plays out way too often. Moving the equipment close to the power outlet will often cause the projected images to be way too small for the audience to view. So, what is to be done? The answer to this question is easy enough: bring your own extension cords. I recommend at least one twenty-five foot extension cord although, personally, I take fifty feet of cord with me just to be on the safe side.

Consider bringing along your own power strip/surge protector—for another practical reason. With a power strip/surge protector available, multiple electronic devices can be plugged right into that, which in turn can be attached to the extension cords. The power surge protection is another benefit. I have conducted book events in historic homes and other older buildings with electrical systems not up to present day electrical wiring standards, placing all electronic devices at great risk. Power strips/surge protectors are inexpensive; you would be wise to invest in one.

◆ Electrical Power/Current Adapters

Authors who plan any type of travel abroad to promote their books must take along electrical power adapters. The standard for electrical current in the United States is 110 volts. In many parts of the world, machines manufactured to operate on 110 volts of electrical current either will not work or could be damaged by the different amounts of electrical current. To make sure the electronic devices work properly and safely, use electrical power/current adapters to regulate the amount of current that will get to electronic devices.

When traveling abroad, you will also discover even the electrical outlets themselves are designed in a different configuration. In most U.S. locations, the power outlets have two parallel slits with a single round hole just below and between them. In many other countries, some outlets are small, round holes, others are configured in more of a triangular pattern, and still others are combinations of shapes. Electronic devices designed for the United States cannot be plugged in unless an adapter is used.

Even in the United States you may go to plug in an electronic device with a three-pronged cord only to discover the venue has the older-style outlets designed for two-pronged cords. If you are not prepared, something as simple as this can ruin a presentation. Therefore, purchase and bring along the adaptor that allows a three-pronged cord to be plugged into a two-pronged outlet—another inexpensive and wise investment.

♦ **Back-up Flash Drive and CD Containing Your Presentation**

Bringing along backups of the presentations is another *must*. For reasons most of us will never understand, laptops and other devices can be quirky at times and simply don't function as we would like. In these cases, you might have to use the equipment at the venue. If the presentation is available on a backup file—both on flash drive and CD—chances are good you can use the host equipment, and the presentation can go on as planned. Of course, you can always switch to an alternate, more low-tech, presentation if necessary. Still, if you have planned on using electronic devices and those devices do not work properly, that could add anxious moments you do not need before an event.

Another practical reason for bringing a back-up of the presentation is that luggage is sometimes lost or misplaced by the airlines. If your electronic devices are in that luggage, a backup of the presentation, on a flash drive or CD, in a carry-on bag can often save the day. I've had this happen to me several times, and having the backup material helped me continue the book events without missing a beat.

♦ Laser Pointer

A laser pointer is a useful tool to help the audience focus upon specific features of the images you wish to emphasize in your presentation. This is especially important when the images are "busy" and contain several objects in the background. Using a laser pointer will also make it easier for you to move around and interact with the audience while speaking because the pointer can be used from any part of the room. Laser pointers are another inexpensive and very good investment if you use a visual presentation.

However, be aware that most airlines, both in the United States and abroad, for security reasons, do not allow laser pointers to be brought aboard the aircraft in carry-on bags. If an author forgets this and accidentally tries to bring one aboard, the laser pointers can be confiscated. It is best to keep them in stowed luggage while traveling. Also, if not used correctly, laser pointers have the potential to cause damage to eyes, both yours and those in the audience. Read the safety precautions and directions for use well in advance of using a laser pointer at an event.

....

A "checklist" of these equipment items that authors can examine before deciding what to take to events can be found in *Appendix B*.

V. Assembling a Publicity Package

Publicity is the name of the game in today's world of book events. Without plenty of advance notice of your book event, whether at bookstores or with special interest groups and organizations, audiences are not going to show up. Therefore, bookstores and other groups will ask you for a comprehensive publicity package to help build the publicity needed to get people to your events. The information in the publicity package will generally be used for posters, fliers, targeted mailings to special customers or members, and press stories/news releases. Those hosting events will also use this information to introduce you to audiences.

You should send the publicity package to bookstores, organizations, and media outlets after a book event has been scheduled. You should provide the following items—and more if requested.

Publicity Photos

Your publicity photos should be in .jpg format, unless otherwise specified by your hosts. These photos should be of very good quality and of high resolution. If possible, send *both* a "head shot" and a "full" shot of you seated or standing in an interesting setting. In addition, the photos should be sent in *both* black and white and color forms so that there will be multiple options for the publicity materials.

The photos should be both "professional" and

"conservative" in tone, unless there is a very special reason for doing otherwise. For instance, if your book is a collection of humorous stories, it *might* be appropriate to send a photo of the author doing something others would find funny or a tad zany. However, conservative photos are *always* appropriate; sending other types of photos can be risky.

It should go without saying, but you also need to make sure what is in the background of the photos is not, in any way, illegal or of such a controversial nature that groups would pull back an invitation. I was once acquainted with an author who kept including a publicity photo showing the author guzzling alcohol in front of a pyramid of empty bottles and cans just in the background. The author thought the picture quite funny; bookstores did not. The author wondered why stores and other groups suddenly made changes to their event schedules, changes that omitted the author.

An Image of Your Book's Cover

An image of the front cover of your book will often be used for a multitude of publicity purposes. Most bookstores, organizations, and media outlets prefer a high-resolution .jpg image, but check with them to find out if they have any specific requirements. This photo should be as clear and detailed as possible. It is also best to send both a color and black and white version of this as well because many newspapers will, because of cost factors, use just the black and white version.

A Short but Interest-catching Book Summary

This summary will be used in the creation of fliers and posters for the event and will also be used by the various media outlets to help with their side of the promotional work. If possible, send multiple summaries, so the different groups can choose the version that best matches their needs and audiences.

Below are sample summaries for one of my recent books, *Ain't No Harm to Kill the Devil: The Life and Legend of John Fairfield, Abolitionist for Hire*. When sending out my publicity package for this book, I sent all of these so that stores and groups could choose the one most appropriate for the specific event.

General Book Summary

Ain't No Harm to Kill the Devil: The Life and Legend of John Fairfield, Abolitionist for Hire, by Jeffrey S. Copeland

◆ Version 1:

One of the most intriguing characters in American history was John Fairfield, an unconventional abolitionist who helped slaves to freedom in the decade before the Civil War. His exploits were cited by Harriet Tubman, Frederick Douglass, and Levi Coffin (the "President" of the Underground Railroad). Sometimes he posed as a land buyer for the railroad, a poultry dealer, a dentist, and even a slaver. One time he led nearly two-dozen slaves to freedom by pretending to be an undertaker taking the body of a slave across the Ohio River to a slave cemetery on the other side! Fairfield was seen by some as a scoundrel, a con man, and a criminal. Others saw him as a religious man who believed that the evils of slavery needed to be wiped away at any cost. In the end, all agreed that Fairfield was successful!

Summaries Written by Reviewers and/or Others

♦ Version 2:

"*Ain't No Harm to Kill the Devil*" is a fast-paced, two-fisted action story with lives full of uncertainty, shadowy subtexts, and hardscrabble realities. Copeland's fiery abolitionist hero, John Fairfield, is a cross between James Bond and John Wayne. With his own licenses to kill (a fire-and-brimstone philosophy, knives, and an 1851 Navy Colt, .31 caliber) Fairfield's covert ops are inventive, full of clever ruses and subterfuge. Fairfield is a patriarchal, self-assured man, with hard-flinted edges. He sees the world in black-and-white terms and uses violence to impose his determined will on the very fabric of America. Copeland's delivered a fascinating piece of Americana. Packs a punch!"

—Grant Tracey, Editor, *North American Review*.

♦ Version 3:

In Jeff Copeland's capable hands, abolitionist John Fairfield rides out of history and into the imagination of today's readers. Subterfuge, disguises, and at times ruthless violence were Fairfield's tools-of-trade as he transported dozens of slaves to freedom in Canada. Fairfield's success spurred enslavers to issue a bounty for his capture. Copeland's nonstop-action narrative sheds important light on a significant historical figure, whose unconventional rescues were a noteworthy force in the abolition movement.

> —Sally M. Walker, author of *Secrets of a Civil War Submarine* and *Boundaries: How the Mason-Dixon Line Settled a Family Feud & Divided a Nation.*

A Short Biography

In addition to its use by the various groups for publicity purposes, your biography will be used by representatives of stores and organizations when you are introduced to the audience before the event. The following is a sample of a recent "author biography" I used in my publicity package. Feel free to use it as a template for creating your own.

> Jeffrey S. Copeland is a professor of English in the Department of Languages and Literatures at the University of Northern Iowa, where he teaches courses in literature and English Education. He has authored numerous books, including *Young Adult Literature: A Contemporary Reader, Inman's War: A Soldier's Story of Life in a Colored Battalion in WWII, Olivia's Story: The Conspiracy of Heroes Behind 'Shelley V. Kraemer',* and *Shell Games: The Life and Times*

of Pearl McGill, Industrial Spy and Pioneer Labor Activist.

If you are preparing for events related to your first book and do not have other titles to mention in the biography, hobbies, activities, and other accomplishments can be listed instead. Some authors actually prefer to have the more personal biography than the more business-like biography. A template for the more personal biography would look something like the following, which you may adapt as is appropriate.

Author Biography Template

(Author's name) currently lives in (town and state), where (he/she) enjoys _____, _____, and _____ (a variety of hobbies and activities would go in the blanks here). (Author's name) is also a graduate of (name of school here), and is a member of (names of organizations and groups here).

Go with the style of biography that feels most appropriate and comfortable for you—because the stores and groups will be happy to have either.

VI. Building an Audience

Of everything you do before a book event, nothing is more important than helping to create an audience. As mentioned previously, the days are gone when bookstores could guarantee a sizable audience by simply taping to their front door a flier announcing an author's appearance. Today, the many ways readers can find out about and purchase books and the changing nature/ roles of bookstores make it essential that authors and bookstores work together to get the word out about book events. As a matter of fact, it is *your responsibility* to work closely with the event coordinators at the stores to help build the audience for the event.

There are many ways you can pitch in and help build an audience. These suggestions will be specifically about preparing for events at bookstores, but the same actions and principles apply if the activity is going to take place for special interest groups or organizations.

Fliers, posters, targeted mailings, and possibly a short notice in the local media were once the most popular methods bookstores used to publicize events. At the same time, authors often relied most heavily upon phone calls and letters to those they knew would be in the immediate area when the event was scheduled to take place. However, communication is much different today, and many other strategies can help make sure an event is well attended.

Digital communication is constantly evolving and will, no doubt, undergo even more changes by the time this manuscript is printed. Every author has a digital footprint of one type or another, depending upon how versed in technology each happens to be. At present, the more popular forms of creating an online digital footprint include the following: Facebook, Snapchat,

Instagram, Tumblr, Reddit, Twitter, Twitch, Vine, LinkedIn, and Pinterest—just to name a few. Not all writers will be connected to each of these digital means of communicating, but most employ at least a couple to help announce everything from immediate to future books and events.

These forms of digital communication are frequently augmented by an author's blog sites and official author websites. Both blogs and websites are ideal locations to announce your upcoming schedule of events. These announcements, which do not have the length restrictions common to traditional media outlets and many electronic means of communication, can provide detailed descriptions and particulars of those events.

Potential readers can easily access the blogs and websites through a host of personal communication devices, ranging from cell phones to tablets to home computers. It is also quite popular now for bookstores and media outlets to direct people to an author's blog and/or author website *specifically to get the more detailed information* about book events they will be hosting. This is one example of bookstores and authors *working together* to get the word out about events.

In addition to these popular electronic announcements, bookstores and authors still need to make use of traditional media outlets. The bookstore or you or both should contact local and regional newspapers to see if there might be opportunities for a feature story about the book/author with information about the event, a small story with the particulars of the upcoming event, or, at the very least, a "public service announcement" posted in the days before and leading up to the event. Many times a bookstore and/or you will not be able to secure all three, but it is very seldom that newspapers will not print at least one piece of information about an upcoming event.

Although more people are gravitating to online newspapers, there is still a significant population of readers who prefer to hold newspapers in their hands. Therefore, if possible, information about events should appear in both forms and in as many newspapers in the town/region as possible. If there are institutions of higher learning in the area—from community colleges to universities—their newspapers should also be contacted. Those newspapers are generally used as "training grounds" for journalism students, and the editors are always on the lookout for stories. They are often quite grateful for the opportunity to have student reporters write up something about the event.

You should also contact local and regional radio and television stations about the possibility of either news stories or announcements about the upcoming event. If they are given enough advance notice and plenty of opportunity for preparation, radio and television representatives are often quite receptive to helping out with the publicity. I recall one particular occasion when I appeared on an early morning television show to talk about my book and the upcoming event. I was happy with the "on air" time and how the program went.

However, it wasn't until I got to the event later that day that I saw just how powerful an influence television can have on the size of an audience. Because of the program, the audience for the book event turned out to be "standing room only," a wonderful problem for a bookstore and author to have.

The same can also be said for local and regional radio stations. Most are quite happy to provide PSA's (Public Service Announcements) about upcoming book events *if* given enough advance notice to fit the announcements into their program schedule. And, you will be pleasantly surprised that radio stations, again if contacted early enough, may allow time for one of their hosts to interview you and/or the bookstore representative about the book and upcoming activity.

Authors and bookstores *must* be aggressive in seeking help from these outlets. Initial contact either via telephone or electronic means with the outlets should take place, at a minimum, four to six weeks before the event is to take place.

At the same time, a traditional "postal mailing" can also be quite useful in announcing an event and helping to generate an audience. One of the most inexpensive and successful means of doing this is by sending specially designed postcards announcing an upcoming event to targeted individuals and specific organizations that might be interested in the event. Many publishers routinely send these out, especially to announce the publication of a new book, but it is always wise for you to consider sending postcards yourself. For those announcing book events, most of the postcards have a nice visual representation of the book—often the book cover—on the front as well as specific information about the time and place of the event. The back is generally reserved for a brief personal note of invitation.

These same postcards with a slight modification help in another important area. By simply removing the specific information about the event, you can send these postcards to bookstores and special groups across the country to announce the release of your new book. Again, the back can be used for a short personal note. Bookstores are constantly bombarded with information about new books, so a personal note of this type can make quite an impression—to your advantage.

Do remember to check with local postal officials about the requirements for the size of the postcards so that extra funds are not required for mailing.

Representative samples of both types of post-cards—to announce events and to announce the release of a book—are listed in *Appendix G*. Feel free to use these as models for creating your own.

Finally, fliers and posters announcing upcoming events are a must. Place these in as many high visibility locations as possible in the area where the event will be taking place. Bookstores and organizations often make all necessary arrangements for these, but there are times when you will have to make fliers and posters yourself. When you find yourself in these situations, a good rule of thumb is to have the following parts on the fliers and posters:

➢ An image of the book cover

➢ A picture of the author

➢ A short description of the book

➢ Name of the bookstore/organization sponsoring the event

➢ Time and location of the event

The posters should be informative but not so long that people will not take the time to read all the way through them. Be specific—but be concise.

Examples of fliers and posters are listed in *Appendix H*. Examine these closely and feel free to use these examples as models for your own posters.

....

When working to build publicity for events, work with the bookstore to target, and get in touch with very specific audiences in both local and surrounding areas. Some of these groups would be the following:

➢ Groups and organizations in the community that would be specifically interested the subject matter or content of the book. For example, when preparing for events for my book *Shell Games*, which deals with the history of the button manufacturing industry in America, I always contacted the local button clubs to let them know about the event. Members of these clubs usually showed up in great numbers at the bookstores. When building publicity for events related to another of my books, *Inman's War*, I always contacted military and veteran groups and invited them to the event. They, too, always seemed to show up in great numbers. Targeting special groups is essential, but the key to success here is to contact those groups through as many means as possible.

➢ As odd as this may sound, you should also contact bookstores other than the one where the event will take place and ask them to help with publicity. Yes, in some respects bookstores are in competition with each other, but those at the bookstores also know that the "brick and mortar" stores are under siege by online retailers. Therefore, sticking together and helping to promote each other is good business sense. What is good for one store is good for *all* stores—to help build a "community" of readers in the area. If there are university bookstores or special-interest bookstores in the area, they, too, should be contacted and asked to help promote the event. They are generally more than happy to lend a hand.

➢ You should also contact local and regional public and private schools. The specific target here would be the level—elementary, middle school/junior high, high school—at which the students would be most interested in the subject matter of the book. Contact here will generally involve two steps. First, you will need to get in touch with the school to ask for permission to send fliers and/or posters to the school. Second, if this permission is granted, you will want to get the names of specific teachers and administrators to whom to send the material about the event. Targeting the individuals who would be most likely to help with the publicity, and most likely to ask students to consider attending the event, is key here. If the specific targeting is not done, it isn't unusual for the publicity materials to end up either in low-visibility places in the school or not posted at all.

➢ Another must is contacting local and regional libraries to ask for their help in promoting the event. Libraries, bookstores, and authors have a special kinship, and all are more than happy to help the others as much as is possible. In the case of libraries, many also have special "reading groups" or "book clubs" that should be invited to attend the event. Again, fliers and posters sent to the libraries can help bring other audiences to the bookstore.

➢ In addition to the "reading groups" and "book clubs" affiliated with libraries, many towns have other book clubs and groups. The library repre-sentatives will also know about these groups and will be happy to share that information. You should then invite those groups to the event.

➢ Many communities also have Writers Groups. Both bookstores and libraries will know about these groups and have very likely worked with them in the past. What better audience for a book event than local authors and aspiring writers? These groups, therefore, should be near the top of the list of those to contact.

> Finally, if the event is to be held anywhere near your "home turf," it should go without saying that you should invite as many relatives, friends, co-workers, and acquaintances as possible. You may feel a tad guilty about doing this, but that should *never* be the case. There is always the chance of the unexpected happening the day of the event that shrinks the number of those who were planning to attend: a sudden change in the weather, a sporting event or community activity rescheduled for that date, a breaking news story that will keep people in front of their computers and televisions.

Because of the unexpected lurking in the wings, it is a blessing to have a "built-in" audience just in case attendance suddenly becomes an issue. Once, even though I had specifically targeted and invited several groups from the local area for a reading and many had indicated they would *definitely* attend, when it was time for the event to begin I saw virtually nothing but friends and relatives before me. After the event I found a strong winter snowstorm had changed direction, and those in the local media urged no travel of any type unless absolutely necessary. My friends and relatives chose to ignore the warnings—thank goodness! Always invite to the events your friends, relatives, and others in your circles. They may be the only ones who show up!

Building an audience is always a challenge. Always

has been—always will be. However, through careful planning and partnering with bookstores to announce the event, you can build good-sized audiences. It takes work—lots of it—but the work will be worth the effort when you see the faces of those eager and waiting to hear about your book.

A checklist of ways to build audiences that you can refer to when preparing for events can be found in *Appendix D.*

Concluding thoughts.....

There are many areas to consider before going out to conduct book readings and events, but attending to each of these can help you achieve the type of success hoped for by all authors. The preparation before events does involve a great amount of work, but this work will pay dividends over and over again as you gain experience with different groups and venues. However, the *before* work is only the beginning, only the foundation for what is to follow: the activities *during* and *after* the events. This additional, and related, work is detailed in the upcoming sections.

SECTION 2

The Essentials to Consider During Book Events

> "I would never read a book if it were possible for me to talk half an hour with the man who wrote it."
> —Woodrow Wilson

Once all the necessary arrangements and preparations have been made *before* a book event is to take place, it is time for you to switch focus to those practices that make the experience *during* your time in front of an audience a success.

Over time, authors will experience all types of venues and audiences. In my case, conducting book events has taken me across the globe and all across America. I've talked about my books everywhere from churches to open fields at festivals to all types of schools to some pretty interesting bookstores. One event was even in an old button factory. All of these experiences have taught me that no matter the audience or venue, I could follow some basic practices that would result in a successful event.

Some of these take time and experience to master, but this is natural and just a part of the process of growing as an author. And, you should find the road to this mastery full of wonderful experiences and a great deal of satisfaction.

The essentials to consider *during the event* fall into seven categories, and each of these will be detailed. Again, my suggestions are geared specifically for events at bookstores, but the same principles apply no matter the speaking venue.

I. Dressing for Success

There has long been a stereotype of what an author should look like. In the past, many expected the author to look cool or trendy. For men, this meant a turtleneck sweater or a dark sport jacket with a black crew shirt underneath. Many expected to see a female author conservatively dressed in a white blouse and sweater—and with a pair of thin reading glasses slid down the nose. What a blessing it is that these stereotypes can be put to rest. Today, the floodgates have opened in terms of what authors can wear to book events, but there are still a few considerations you should keep in mind. Your clothing choice *does* make a difference.

First, "business casual," for both men and women, is nearly always appropriate attire for book readings and events. This has become popular for several reasons. It is easy to pack suitable "business casual" clothing in suitcases if you are going to be traveling any distance to an event. This type of clothing is also comfortable, which is important since you are likely to be standing and performing in front of audiences for long periods of time. If media outlets come to events, that manner of dress will always be appropriate for their photographs. In addition, many who purchase books will want their pictures taken with you while the book is being signed. You will also want photographs that can be used for your blog sites and websites.

Another consideration here is the color of your clothing. Both newspaper photographers and television producers prefer that authors wear darker clothing. The darker clothing appears much more "defined" and provides better contrast against backdrops in pictures; lighter clothing tends to "wash out" and blend into the background. Many authors soon learn it is a bad idea all around to wear light-colored clothing because of how quickly these can appear dirty, wrinkled, and worn. A random ink mark, a food stain, dust from brushing against a dusty door or wall, will all show up, unfortunately, if you wear light-colored clothing.

Finally, the specific venue should also be taken into consideration. One might wish to dress more formally if speaking in front of a corporate group or at a national conference. At the same time, more casual attire might be the order of the day if speaking to a small special interest group. The final choice is always up to you, but do remember it is always better to overdress than to discover your clothing is out of place.

II. Arriving at the Event

When you first arrive, immediately check in with the event coordinator. This is not only correct but polite because it allows the event coordinator finally to exhale and relax some. If unforeseen circumstances cause you to be late—or even worse to not show up—think of the problems that can cause those at the store. Therefore, announce your presence as soon as possible.

In addition, experienced authors will nearly all agree on this point: Get to the event early! A good rule of thumb is to arrive thirty to forty-five minutes before the activities are to begin. There are several reasons for this.

If you use any technology in presentations—from Powerpoint to audio clips—there will be times when technical problems arise. When setting up equipment for a book event, I've discovered nonfunctioning electrical outlets in the room. I've had the electronic equipment at the stores not be compatible with my materials. I've had bulbs in projectors suddenly burn out the second the device was turned on. I've shown up expecting to find a projection screen, only to discover the group hosting the event forgot to secure one. All of these were significant problems, but with enough time to devote to solutions before the events were to begin, I was able to take care of most of the issues before the last of the audience arrived. I always get to book events at least forty-five minutes early just in case some "surprises" are lurking.

Also, you do not want the audience watching you set up the equipment. Have everything up and running with your title slide on the screen before your audience arrives. If you are using a microphone or sound system, make the time for some testing and practice to be sure all is in order. To put this into perspective, just how many people would really want to watch Rembrandt clean brushes before starting on a painting?

Another important reason for arriving early has to do with inspecting *where* the event will take place in the bookstore or other venue. The specific location where you will be speaking can be key to your success. Unless absolutely necessary, you should not speak in front of a door because of the disruption of people coming in and out of the space. The best scenario is to have a wall or partition behind you for sound projection and distribution. Many of those in charge of events place a table or podium just in front of a store's door or entrance to help attract more people for the audience. This is sound reasoning but, practically, you will be difficult to hear if placed in such a location. If you get to an event early and see such an arrangement, suggest politely and respectfully that the position of the podium or table be changed. Once your reason for wanting the reconfiguration of the space is heard, most often the room will be reorganized.

You should also not assume the space for the event will be set up with chairs and tables when you arrive. Bookstores are busy places, and those who work there often have a difficult time getting free from their regular duties to prepare the space for the event. If you show up early and offer to help with the set-up, those at the bookstore will be most appreciative. While helping out, suggest that the chairs *not* be put into evenly-spaced, symmetrical rows, all facing the podium or where you will be standing. This is the way chairs were configured in school, where people were told to sit quietly. Stagger the chairs so that the rows are somewhat irregular. This arrangement will not only help people in the audience see around those in front of them, but it will affect the whole atmosphere of the room.

Finally, the location where you will be signing books at the end of the event is often in a separate room or space. If you arrive early enough, you can also help with the set-up of the signing table and make sure time does not have to be devoted to that later on. If this is *not* done in advance, those who wish to purchase the book and have it signed will have to wait in line potentially a great deal of time while the set-up takes place, which just might cause them to leave early.

"Location, location, location" is important when considering where the event will take place in the bookstore. By arriving early, you can help take care of issues that might make the location less than ideal.

III. Building Rapport with the Audience

The plain, simple fact of the matter is that some authors are more comfortable in front of audiences than others. Some are natural-born speakers who enliven a room full of people the minute they open their mouths and enjoy their experience in front of groups. Others, many of whom are wonderfully gifted writers, would rather be doing just about anything other than standing in front of a podium, and they really have to work to engage an audience. However, no matter your disposition or desires in this area, getting "out there" to promote a book is a must for almost every author. Sales of some books take off incredibly from the minute they are published—and the authors don't need to do much promotion. However, for the rest of us—and that is most of us—meeting readers and speaking to audiences is just part of being a writer.

While time and experience are the great teachers in learning how to engage an audience, you can also take a few steps when you share yourself and your book with an audience to help make a successful and enjoyable experience for all involved. Build rapport with your audience through the following steps.

Make a Positive First Impression

Always remember that you are selling yourself just as much as your book, so a good first impression upon the audience is a *must*. After getting all equipment ready and setting up the signing table, and while waiting for the event to start, visit with those who come early. Do not be shy and just sit there. Initiate conversations. Ask them questions about the local community. Ask how long they've been patrons of the store or members of the group being addressed and what they like most about it. Ask what types of books they enjoy—and about the last book they read.

Before I go to bookstores to do events, I always read through the local newspapers to see if I can find any interesting items in the news; then I ask those who come early what their feelings are about the topic. This may seem like idle conversation—and in some ways it is—but it serves to break the ice and help establish that you are interested in *them* and *their community*, which is a nice way to begin establishing rapport. This will also help chase off a case of "butterflies" because you have already engaged several in the crowd.

Build Rapport with Opening Remarks

When it is finally time to start your presentation, choose your opening carefully. In the past, authors often told a joke to break the ice and begin the event. This is not so much the case today. Jokes are simply too risky and have the potential to offend members of the audience. Instead, begin simply and easily by including the following right at the start of your talk.

Thank You!

When you are introduced to the audience, give an enthusiastic "thank you" to the event coordinator and/or other individuals hosting the event. Point them out to the audience and ask everyone there to help thank them for their work. (A little applause goes a long way.) Hosting a book event is incredibly time-consuming, so a thank you to those involved is always appropriate—and appreciated.

Next, be sure to thank those in the audience for being there. Always remember there are plenty of other things they could be doing, but they chose to be there with you. Therefore, they, too, are deserving of thanks.

Support the Store

Say something positive about the bookstore—and how pleased you are to be there. Comment upon the layout of the store, its location, the range of titles on the shelves, its importance to the community, and so forth. Let those in the local area know what a treasure they have in the bookstore. With the number of brick-and-mortar stores shrinking, let everyone know how important it is to support them.

Can You Hear Me?

Always ask if those in the back and off to the sides can hear you. They won't speak up if they can't, so you'll have to ask. If this is a problem, adjust the sound system or move closer to the audience. Don't just speak louder. Do everything you can, from moving chairs around to moving yourself around, to make sure all can enjoy the presentation. The audience will appreciate your effort to make sure all will be able to interact in the event, which helps build positive rapport.

Set the Mood with an Anecdote

Humor is the universal glue at events of this type, but you do not have to be a comedian to engage an audience. If you can incorporate humor, that's great. If something humorous doesn't come to mind, then something "interesting" will be just as effective. Before getting to your book, begin with a *short* anecdote or amusing story about your travel there or your preparation for the event. If possible, share something about a link or connection you might have with the local area or region—again to help establish rapport with those in attendance. The audience came to meet you and hear about your book, so don't drag this out. Still, if possible, find something that you can share either about you or your book that will help establish a positive atmosphere in the room.

Once, while entering England to give a talk about one of my books, I was detained by Customs because I looked like a "person of interest" they were watching for. I actually had to give the first few minutes of my talk for the book event before the Customs officials were convinced I was an author and let me go. Later, at the event, I shared this with the audience as soon as I was introduced, and those in the room erupted in laughter. After that, the atmosphere was such that the talk went as smooth as could be. At another event, I mentioned at the very beginning I had been through the town many times before and had always stopped by a particular bakery for the best pie I'd ever had (I checked before the event, and the bakery was still there)—and asked those in the audience if we should send someone to get a few pies for us to eat while I spoke to them. We didn't send for the pies, but many in the room nodded their heads and others smiled, which helped us make an immediate connection.

A template for the "opening" remarks during a presentation can be found in *Appendix E.*

Bring "Giveaways"

At the start of events, few things can bring smiles more quickly to the faces of those in the audience than "giveaways." People *love* getting something for free. At book events, the giveaway" items do not have to be elaborate or expensive. The free items, no matter what they are, serve as a nice way of connecting you to the audience—and the audience to the book. The giveaway you use should be related somehow to the subject matter, theme, or content of the book. The more traditional giveaways are bookmarks and postcard-sized pictures having something to do with the book and often an image of the front cover. These are always appropriate, but some lean more toward the creative side here. They give out inexpensive ink pens or pencils with the title of the book printed on them. Others bring small booklets, usually with additional information inside about the book or how it came about. Still others give out nicely-printed cards with the author's blog, website, and contact information.

My own experience with giveaways has always been positive—because of the immediate connection they help make between the audience and the book and how they create a positive and fun atmosphere in the room. For many events involving my book *Shell Games*, the major setting of which was the early button manufacturing industry, I brought bags of buttons and handed out a few to each who entered the presentation space. I told each to hang onto them, and I'd explain their significance during the reading. Many laughed while receiving the buttons, and that was exactly the response I was aiming for. The buttons were later excellent "visual aids" during my presentation when I described the early button manufacturing process.

For *Ain't No Harm to Kill the Devil*, I have given out postcard-sized "wanted posters" of the main character, John Fairfield. Again, I told everyone they would understand the importance of the poster after hearing about Fairfield's life. With audience curiosity working overtime, the presentation flowed smoothly.

For *Olivia's Story*, I gave everyone bookmarks with a photo of the main characters who did not appear in the "Photo" section of the book. Later, during the reading, I asked those in the audience to look at the picture while I read a section of the story that related directly to the new photo. Those in attendance felt they were getting something "extra" that other readers couldn't.

The giveaways are an effective, and fun, way to help establish an immediate rapport and connection with your audience. You do not have to use giveaways, but you should at least consider experimenting with them to see if the results work well. Remember, too, when giveaways are taken out of the store, promotion of the book goes on as people tell others about them. Also, if you use giveaways, bookstores will appreciate it if you leave a few behind that can be given to those who later purchase the book.

Appoint an "Official" Photographer

It is usually a good idea to have pictures taken at your book events. You can use these photos to update blogs and websites—and to help chronicle your experiences while on the road. The photos can also be used to create future promotional materials. Since it is not practical for you to take the pictures while speaking, you will need to enlist someone else to help with this. As another way of helping build rapport with the audience, you should ask someone in the group to be the "official photographer"—and then give that person a camera to use. The person chosen is usually more than happy to serve in this role and enjoys helping out.

Ask the "official photographer" to take a fair number of pictures during the event. Pause at times and thank the photographer for the assistance. At the end of events, I always ask everyone else in the room to give the photographer a round of applause. Again, having someone help with the pictures achieves two goals. You build rapport with the audience, and you end up with a record of the event, which can later be used for multiple purposes.

Bring Food

While not as popular as it once was, many authors still like to bring some type of food to share with members of the audience. Today, if you wish to do this, first ask the event coordinator if the rules of the bookstore allow for food. Bringing food is strictly forbidden by many stores, and they can't be faulted for this. After all, when food is involved, the potential for messes is great. In addition, leftover food might draw in multiple-legged "critters" of various types, which can be quite a serious situation in a room full of books.

If food is allowed, and if it is practical for you to bring it along, sharing food can be another means of bringing you and your audience together. Some authors like to bring candy, cookies, or other small treats. Others bring food that is somehow, even if in a small way, related to the subject or content of the book. For example, a book event I've never forgotten was one at which the author brought in a small wedding cake and served a slice to everyone in the audience. This fit perfectly as her book was a collection of short stories about the joys of married life.

If you can't think of a particular type of food that matches something in the book, a nice alternative exists, an alternative I've chosen to use many times. If I do not have to travel a great distance for an event, or will be in an area for at least a couple of days, I'll often have a bakery make a special cake I can share with the audience. Most bakeries are able to reproduce the front cover of the book on the icing on the top of the cake. In order to make these cakes, the bakeries will need a clean, high-resolution photograph of the front cover of your book. It is best to make this photocopy on standard eight and a half by eleven-inch paper. I bring these cakes to events, and offer everyone "a piece of the book." I'm always amazed by how relaxed the atmosphere in the room becomes when the book is talked about while people are enjoying the cake. Enjoying cake together is just another means of building rapport with an audience you should keep as a possibility.

Finally, if you bring food, keep in mind a few other "rules" related to bringing food to an event. First, you—not the bookstores—are responsible for bringing paper plates, napkins, and eating utensils. After the event, you should help with the clean-up of the space if that is needed. Also, any food that has not been eaten should be left for those who work at the bookstore; they will appreciate this very much.

Building rapport and connection with the audience is not difficult to do, but you must make a concerted effort and build the effort right into the presentation. With a little time and practice, building rapport will become second nature.

IV. Interacting with the Audience During Events

Everything an author can do to help build rapport with the audience goes hand-in-hand with the interaction *while* the event is taking place. Authors who have the most success in front of groups engage and draw the audience members into the presentation. A presentation/reading should not have a strict lecture format in which you are the only one who speaks. In other words, the event should not be like a class in school. Those in the audience should be encouraged at various points to contribute to your presentation. In order to get as many people involved as possible, consider the following suggestions.

Make Eye Contact

Make eye contact with *everyone* in the room. Most speakers tend to favor one side of the room over the other. Some research indicates a person's "dominant hand" has something to do with this, but it is likely more than that. The side of the room where lecterns and tables are placed plays a significant role in how speakers interact with groups and where focus in placed. No matter the reason, you must draw in *both* sides of the audience so people do not feel excluded. Some authors go so far as jotting a note in the margin of their presentation notes to remember to involve both sides of the room.

Enhance the Discussion

Stop at various points in the event and present a "scenario" to the audience. The scenario should be a discussion point that has something to do with the main events being talked about from the book. This could be why a certain character behaved as he/she did. It could be asking the audience members what they would have done in a similar situation compared to what those in the book did. It could be asking what other course of action could have been taken in a specific scene. Of course, the type of book will determine what scenarios to include, but virtually every book has sections in it that can be used for discussion purposes.

Many authors, myself included, like to ask those in the audience to pair up and discuss these scenarios. Then, after a few minutes, different pairs from around *both* sides of the room can share their thoughts and feelings about the matter at hand. This is a good way to get the audience fully engaged in the presentation.

Pause for Questions

It is easy to be "on a roll" and forget to pause to see if those in the audience have questions about the presentation. This is another area where many authors jot reminders to do this in their presentation notes. Individuals in the audience don't raise hands all that often to ask questions, even if they are sitting there with several they are thinking about. Therefore, authors should pause at times, look at the audience (both sides of the room!), and ask if anyone has a question to ask. Wait at least a good thirty seconds or so to see if hands go up because people are generally very shy about asking the first question.

Build in Questions

If there are no immediate questions asked, an effective way of getting a discussion started is to give out questions to be asked. Before each event, prepare questions that you would like to discuss. These can be written on file cards or printed on regular paper. Give these to members of the audience—then ask them to pose the question either to the rest of the group or you. Those in attendance usually find this amusing. When I use the prepared questions, I always walk into the audience and shake the hands of those who ask the questions and say, "That was a great question!"—which brings smiles to the faces of those all around.

Prepare for the Standard Questions from Audiences

Once an audience gets involved in the presentation, there are "old stand-by" questions that nearly always seem to pop up in one form or another. You should have carefully thought out and have prepared detailed responses to these so you can make additional connections with the audience. These "old stand-by" questions are typically as follows:

- ➤ How did you come up with the title of your book?
- ➤ How long did it take you to write the book?
- ➤ What advice do you have for beginning writers? (You should be careful with this one; a few sage words of advice are fine, but remember the focus at the event should be on *your book* and getting it sold.)
- ➤ Which authors have influenced you the most?
- ➤ Where do you do your writing?
- ➤ Which authors do you most admire, and why? (Again, you should be careful here. The focus should be on *you* and your book.)
- ➤ What have you been reading lately?
- ➤ Why should I buy your book? (People actually ask this, so be prepared with your best sales pitch.)
- ➤ What's your next book going to be about? (In some cases, you may not wish to give away specifics of a work in progress, for the obvious reasons. If that is the case, let them know the *type* of book it will be instead—mystery, biography, poetry, science fiction, and so on.)
- ➤ Where is the favorite place you've visited while doing book signings?

Again, these questions, and variations of them, will invariably be posed by those in the audience at one event or the other. Responses prepared in advance will help keep the flow of the presentation going smoothly—and will impress those in the room. And, if the discussion is slow and these questions aren't asked, remember you can have these written out on cards or slips of paper and give them out to members of the audience—and these can help initiate good discussion in a group.

Dealing with "Hecklers" and "Critics"

It very seldom happens, but someone in the audience may make a negative comment about something in your book: "I didn't like the way the main character was presented." "I didn't care for the structure of the book." "The ending just didn't seem right." Do *not* be confrontational with these people. All are allowed an opinion about the work, and you have to respect that. It is best to politely thank them for their views and mention that writers have many choices to make, in style and structure, when putting a book together. A comment of this type does not mean you are agreeing with the person; it simply means you respect the point of view. Then, you should immediately move the discussion to another area—and toward something more positive.

You will seldom, if ever, really know why these individuals feel as they do about the book. Therefore, let them express their views, acknowledge them, and move on without letting the comments rattle you. If you don't respond badly to the negative comments, others in the audience will have just that much more respect for you and what you create.

V. Signing Your Book

Event coordinators will ask you to do one of two things: Have either a book reading/event *and* a signing, or do just the book signing without the presentation. Some stores simply do not have the space for large events, so they will prefer to have you stop in to meet informally with patrons and sign books. The "signing only" event does not take as much time and effort to prepare for and promote. At times, you may prefer the signing-only event, especially if several events have been scheduled in a short period of time. The main disadvantage to the signing-only event is that you do not get much time to interact with the readers and discuss the book, especially if the line of those waiting to purchase the book is long. Still, the signing-only events can be a rewarding experience.

On the other hand, the bookstore may want you to do both a reading/presentation and a book signing session. In this case, the bookstores will typically set up a special table where you can sign books and visit with patrons after completing the main presentation.

No matter which type of event is to take place, the same "Book Signing Basics" apply.

The Signing Table

Work with the event coordinator to make sure the signing table is eye-catching and functional. First, make sure plenty of copies of your book are neatly stacked on the table. This is very important because nothing kills the mood of those in line like having to wait a long time for more books to be brought out from a storeroom or off the shelves. If there is enough room, it is a good idea to store the extra books under the table but away from your feet, so they don't accidentally get knocked over.

Your bookmarks, business cards, blog and website information, and other related items should be neatly arranged on the table. It's a good idea to place these at the far end of the table so people can pick them up *after* their books are signed—to help keep the line moving.

Also, bring framed pictures of yourself, the book cover, and, if you wish, other photos that reflect the subject or content of the book. These should be small (five by seven or eight by ten at the largest). Place these around the table. These extra pictures help for two reasons. First, many purchasing your book will want a picture taken with you, and these framed pictures will help provide a nice background for the pictures. Second, if you are doing a presentation in another section of the building, those entering the store will see the signing table and, if it appears interesting enough, some might just decide to come to the event. Thus, the table actually becomes a promotional advertisement for you and the work. Also, have one or two of those in line use your camera to take a picture of you seated at the table and interacting with others. These pictures can be used for blog sites, websites, and other ways the book is being promoted.

The Store Signing Policies

Always check with the store to find out the policy about *when* books can be signed. Some stores require people to purchase the book *before* it can be signed. There is a good logic to this policy. Some individuals get books signed—and then discover they have left all means of payment at home. In some cases, rather than having the bookstore hold the book until the person can get back with payment, the book is left somewhere in the store. It is mighty difficult to sell a book signed for "Karrryn" to anyone else.... Other bookstores allow individuals to have the book signed first and then move to a register to pay for it. It is your responsibility to check with the store to learn about the specific policy followed there.

How Is Your Name Spelled?

Always ask those who would like to have their books signed how their names are spelled! I cannot emphasize this enough. If you do not ask for the correct spelling and use an incorrect one, the purchaser of the book will either be disappointed or refuse to take the book alto-gether, which would be his/her right. Trying to correct a wrong spelling that was done in ink can lead to quite a mess. If the person will not accept the book with a name marked out and the correct spelling placed above, most often you will be responsible for paying for the book.

This is such a problem because there are so many variations of the spelling of names, and you are only "guessing" if you do not ask up front. Over the past couple of years, I have signed for a Karrryn (3 r's), Gohn (pronounced "John"), Fillyp (another version of "Phillip"), Kacciee (pronounced "Casey"), Miikkee (pronounced "Mickey"), and Allycee (pronounced "Alice"). You will quickly learn that there is no standard spelling of a name.

Most authors either ask those in line to write their names on a slip of paper while they are waiting—or ask them when they get to the table, "How would you like this signed?" Once the name has been given, it is appropriate to ask, "And how is that spelled?" People are not offended by these questions. On the contrary, they are pleased the author cares enough to make sure all is correct. If the name is also spelled differently from what you were expecting, it is also an opportunity to ask how that particular spelling came about. Some pretty interesting stories come out of those discussions.

Book Inscriptions

Equally important to asking for the correct spelling for names, you should come up with and practice, in advance of the event, at least two or three short inscriptions (sentences or phrases) that can be used when signing the books. If you have more than one title for sale at an event, have different inscriptions for each. Quite simply, most readers love inscriptions to go along with your signature. Writing "For (the person's name)," followed by a simple "Enjoy!" or "Happy Reading!"—or something similar—followed by your signature will be enough, especially if the line of those waiting for a book is quite long.

However, if possible, a short inscription related somehow to the book is preferred. For example, for my book *Olivia's Story*, I often used this inscription, followed by my signature: "I hope you enjoy this story of a band of unsung American heroes!" For *Shell Games*, I frequently used the following inscription: "Mystery, mayhem, and murder await—read this with the lights on!" Inscriptions should also be short and easy to write because of the time it takes to put them to paper and will vary depending on the time you can spend with each reader.

Keep Up a Good Pace!

There will often be "talkers" and others who "gum-up" the line. Of all the problems that can occur during the signing process, this is potentially one of the most serious. If the wait for a signature is too long, many choose to give up and leave the store, often without purchasing the book. Therefore, when a reader has remained in front of you an inordinate amount of time, you have a couple of choices. First, you can politely tell the reader that there are many others in line and you need to meet them as well. If the person still does not move along, you can ask the person to do a favor—like getting the manager so more books can be brought to the table, or finding someone who works at the store so that the thermostat can be changed to make the room warmer/ cooler, or even asking the person to step to the side to take a picture of you signing for the next person. These "favors" may sound somewhat devious—and they are— but if the line comes to a screeching halt, those who are still waiting for signatures are going to get mighty hot— even if it is cool in the room.

When Lines Slow Down

At slow times, when there isn't a line of those waiting for a signature, don't just sit there behind the table. Use the time to tidy-up and rearrange everything from bookmarks to pictures. After doing that, move out in front of the table and introduce yourself to those passing by. Ask if they'd like to hear about your book. If you brought treats to the event (cake, cookies, candy), ask if they'd like some to help you celebrate the publication of your book. Also, if they have the time, ask them to take a picture of you at the signing table so you can use it later for your blog and website. This request can lead to additional conversation—and possibly a purchase of the book. If nothing else, be sure they take a bookmark or other promotional piece with them so they can find out more information about the book later on. It's a pretty sad picture when an author just sits at the table and waits for readers to come over. Keep visiting with others and promoting yourself in all ways possible.

VI. Wrapping Up the Event

After the book signing period is over and the last of those in the audience have gone, you still have much to do before leaving the store.

Signing Extra Books

Ask the event coordinator if you can sign the rest of the books that did not sell. The gesture will be greatly appreciated. Most stores have "Author Signed" stickers to put on the front covers of books. Often, the fact that a book has been signed by the author will help sell it. Also, if the books are signed, the bookstore will not likely send unsold copies back to the publisher or distributor but will keep them on the shelves to sell.

Offer Your Assistance

Ask if you can help rearrange chairs and tables that have been moved for the event. If you don't help with this, those at the bookstore carry the whole burden of getting the store back to normal. Again, your offer may be turned down, but the gesture will be remembered. Also, ask if there is anything else you can help with while there. For instance, quite often bookstores will have "albums" of one type or another they have authors sign who do events at their store—so that these can be made available for customers to browse through. If the store has an album, be sure to sign it before leaving—and

include in it your comments and your thanks to the
event coordinator and others at the store.

Leave Giveaways

If you brought giveaways, leave some of these at the
store so they can be given to those who purchase the
book later on. Stores very much appreciate having some
of these to give to their customers.

Obtain Copies of Publicity Materials

Ask if you can take at least one copy of any fliers and
posters the bookstore used to help promote the event.
These can later be studied and used when other publicity materials are created. Many writers keep something
of a scrapbook of these materials—both to keep a record
of the events and as a storehouse of ideas for future promotional materials.

A Final Thank You to All

Before leaving the store, once again thank the event
coordinator and everyone else at the store who helped
out with the event. Many authors, sadly, don't show
their appreciation for all the work that went into getting
the store ready for the event. It takes a few minutes, so
make the time to give one more round of thanks.

Be Mindful of Security

For security reasons, always ask either the event coordinator or another member of the bookstore staff to escort you outside to your vehicle. Ask for this no matter where the event is being held and no matter the time of day or night. Overzealous "fans" and other individuals can cause problems, of multiple types, in parking lots. Plus, if you brought equipment with you, you will need help carrying everything out to the vehicle so you do not have to make multiple trips. Do not ignore the old advice, "There is safety in numbers."

VII. Make Some Time for Yourself!

One of the true perks of being an author is being able to travel to so many different places and being able to explore the local and surrounding areas while there. You may already know of interesting sites before going to a town, but if you do not, ask those at the bookstores and those in the audiences for recommendations of "must-see" places. Typically, the locals will be able to recommend the more "out of the way" places of interest that tourists very seldom find out about. I always love to visit historic sites and businesses, other booksellers, and local restaurants and bakeries. I always check to see if there are special tours available for the town so I can get a sense of the area's history. The places you visit and the people you meet along the way will provide cherished memories. As always, be sure to have a good camera close by. Photographs from the trip might be appropriate to post on author blog sites and websites to keep readers up-to-date on your activities.

The primary purposes of going out to do book events are to sell audiences on the book and you. At the same time, you can have the most wonderful experiences while on the road. Because of my books, I've been able to visit countries I never otherwise would have seen. While conducting events at bookstores and with other groups, I've met some of the most interesting people I've ever known. Being a successful author takes a lot of hard work and dedication, but through that work, so many great experiences will open up before you. Therefore, while traveling to do book events, *make the time* to enjoy the travel and the places you see and the people you meet. Those are the true hidden treasures of being an author that you will remember forever.

Concluding thoughts.....

Your activities *during* a book event can make the experience both exciting and memorable for everyone, including you. Following these suggestions will put a good foundation in place to help build the confidence you must have when standing in front of an audience. Once you are comfortable with this foundation, each event will become another building block in helping you achieve your goals and objectives in sharing books with audiences.

SECTION 3

Activities for Consideration After Events:

> *"Great is the art of beginning, but greater is the art of ending."*
> —Henry Wadsworth Longfellow

Your work is not finished *after* book events have taken place—far from it. The post-event activities are just as important as those taken care of *before* and *during*. If anything, many of the *after* activities continue building success upon success—and help prepare you for future events. You should take care of some of these activities *immediately* after events. Others are "on-going" and help maintain publicity and promotional materials.

I. Sending Thank You Notes

Immediately after the event, send "Thank You" notes to the event coordinator and everyone else at the bookstore who helped arrange and carry out the event. It takes a tremendous amount of work to make ready a

book event, so make the time to show your appreciation for their efforts. Special "Thank You" cards are
always appropriate. Or, if you prefer, a short letter will
also suffice. Offering thanks for help is common courtesy, but there is another reason this is important. You
want those at the bookstore to remember how appreciative you were the *next* time you have a book published. Gratitude given now can help pave the way for
invitations for future events—and that should never be
forgotten.

Somewhere in your "Thank You" note—or in a separate message—let those at the bookstore know you will
be happy to provide "personalized notes and your signature" for those who purchase your book(s) after the
event is over. This is actually quite easy, and inexpensive, to do. Bookplates with adhesive backs are readily
available from print shops and online retailers. Basically,
bookplates are "stickers" large enough for a short note
and your signature. Simply let the bookstore representatives know you are willing to personalize bookplates
for those who purchase the book—and that all they
will need to do is send you the correct spelling of the
names. Once you have those names, it is a simple matter
to write the person's name, use one of the inscriptions
you've prepared for the book, sign your name, and then
send the bookplate back to the bookstore—where it
will be given to the customer. Bookstores will be most
appreciative of your willingness to do this, especially if
many of their regular customers could not make it to
your event. Being able to acquire the personalized note

and your signature will leave the reader quite impressed with both the bookstore and you.

II. Checking Back with Bookstores

On a regular basis, visit the bookstores in your town or immediate area to see if they have received new copies of your books that they would like to have signed. Again, author-signed books sell very well, so this extra effort on your part will be greatly appreciated. While you are at the store, it is also nice to touch base with the event coordinator—and thank the individual again for selling your books. Bookstores have only so much shelf space, so you should be grateful for their help. Also, bring along another batch of bookmarks or other items that you routinely give out at book events so that these can be given to those who purchase the books. While you are there, ask if there is anything else you can do to help the store. They might be putting up a special display of some type, and you could help with that. They might be having a "story hour" going on, and you could also help out there. Bookstores are active, vibrant places, and authors who are willing to help out there are much appreciated.

III. Filling In

When you visit the bookstores, there is something else you can volunteer to do to endear yourself to those there. There are times when, because of everything from travel glitches to illness, authors cannot make it to scheduled events that have been publicized for weeks—or possibly even months. If an author cancels, what is the bookstore to do? Here is where you can help out. If you live within easy travel from the bookstore, let the event coordinator know that if your schedule would permit it, you'd be willing to fill in for an author who cannot make it to an event. It wouldn't be the same as having the original author speak to the group, but last-minute changes like this are difficult for stores to communicate to customers. And, some people get quite upset when they take the time from their schedules to get to the advertised event, only to find out nothing is taking place at the store. Having a back-up speaker who can fill in at a moment's notice can be a blessing for a bookstore. A good number of those who write also love meeting with audiences. If you are one of those writers, volunteer to do this if the bookstores get in a pinch.

IV. Scouting Potential Resources

While traveling to do book events, make the time to scout out potential sources of assistance with your writing and your promotional work. There might be special libraries, archives, or records centers in the area that could help you with future research for a book. There might be other bookstores you've never visited before, and these might turn out to be appropriate venues for your events. You might even find a special place for inspiration and writing. I've found several such locations during my travels, and I now frequent them when I have a book project.

V. Maintaining an Online Presence

Maintain and update author blog sites, websites, and all other means used to communicate with readers. Blog sites and websites are two of the more useful means of keeping readers in touch with current events and upcoming projects, so devote special attention to both. Blog sites are generally very easy to update, and many authors make the time to update not just when they are home but when they are on the road. Make sure to have your blog site password within easy reach just in case you wish to make an announcement while moving from event to event. At the same time, make sure you always have a camera with you that you can use to upload pictures to the site.

Author websites are not as easy to update. As a matter of fact, they can be downright difficult to work with. Still, if they are regularly maintained, these can be a great source of information for readers about you and your work and travels. The key to success with an author website is having one that is structured appropriately and has available on it the "typical" pieces of information that readers particularly enjoy browsing through. Therefore, the website should also be *very* easy to navigate. For many, getting the initial author website in place is a difficult task. To make this process easier, a checklist of the areas to include on the site can be found in Appendix F. The checklist should help you build the initial site—and help make it practical and functional.

A note of caution: Give careful consideration to listing the dates of upcoming events on all electronic means of communicating with your readers. This is routinely done and does help considerably with promotion of events. However, this same knowledge will also let people know when you will not be at your home. Therefore, if upcoming event dates are listed, make sure appropriate security measures are in place to minimize the potential for robberies and other issues at your home.

VI. Participating in Online Sales

There are many camps debating what online booksellers are doing to the publishing world and whether this influence is positive or negative. Some groups, to varying degrees, believe online booksellers will eventually eliminate the need for brick-and-mortar stores and will then have the power to regulate and control what does and does not get published. At the other end of the spectrum are those who believe the "online book evolution/revolution" is a bonanza for new writers because of the vast opportunities for publication that aren't always there through the traditional publishers.

However, a simple fact cannot be ignored. In recent years, e-book sales of have overtaken hardcover sales and are catching up on paperback sales—and that trend is likely to continue as more electronic devices appear that allow readers to purchase and read books. Therefore, this debate will, no doubt, continue to grow and evolve through the years. Right now, however, you must decide just how much you wish to participate in the online sales of your books. If you are going to be involved, there are very specific sites you must create; for example, an "Amazon Author Central" page would be one of these. At the same time, for these to be effective and help with the promotion of you and your work, they need to be regularly maintained.

In the end, you must decide for yourself what is best. This decision will not be an easy one because authors must consider that e-book sales have the potential to cause financial harm to brick-and-mortar stores, especially the independent booksellers—because in most cases they stand to gain very little, if anything, from e-sales.

VII. Keeping Files

Maintain a file for each book published. These files should contain everything from copies of reviews, to posters/fliers used to announce book events, to photographs related to your work at events. These files will be invaluable as you create and design future promotional materials.

VIII. Going Video

One of the best ways to promote a new book is by creating a *YouTube* video (or similar video platform). Use the video to give a summary of the work, to give some information about how the book came to be written, and to provide a "teaser" that will make the viewers want to purchase the book. *YouTube* videos are not difficult to make; there are dozens of sites on the Internet that provide step-by-step instructions.

The greatest value of these videos is that they can be linked to most electronic means of communication you use. Because the promotional worth of these videos cannot be underestimated, you should experiment with them. Start small—create a very short, one or two minute "booktalk" about your new book. Post the video, link it to your means of communicating with readers, and evaluate the results of your efforts. You may find this method of promoting yourself and your work will be quite effective.

IX. Maintaining Correspondence

Responding to letters and notes from readers is an important part of the life of an author. Most of this type of communication has shifted to the electronic world, but the amount of "regular" mail you receive could be significant, especially shortly after the release of a new book. Whether the readers send regular mail or electronic notes, you should do your very best to acknowledge these in some fashion. Several of my writer friends receive so many pieces of communication from readers they've had to enlist the aid of others to help with the response. What a wonderful problem to have! However, most of us do not get nearly that volume, so it is up to us to create an effective, and efficient, means of response.

It may not be practical to send a personal response to everyone who writes; therefore, you might consider using a "standard" response note that can be adapted, as needed, for individual readers. Such a response does not have to be long. As a matter of fact, most of the "standard" responses have just two parts: 1) Thank the person for writing, and 2) Tell how much it means to you that your book was enjoyed. When I receive these letters, I also like to include with my response a bookmark or one of my author business cards. Readers appreciate these acknowledgments. Below is a sample of a "standard" note you can use and adapt as appropriate.

"Thank you for your very kind note. I'm so happy you enjoyed my book. I had a great time putting it together, and it is pretty wonderful for an author to discover the words also mean something to someone else. Again, thank you for making the time to write to me. I appreciate that very much! Sincerely, _____"

If you receive a large amount of mail, a note of this type printed out on notecards, and then personally signed to the reader, will also suffice. I recommend keeping the "standard" reply in a special file so it is handy when the letters come to you.

X. Attending Others' Book Events

It is often said that experience is the best teacher. For authors, this is very much true in the area of book events, and one of the best ways to gather this experience is to attend as many book events as possible to see what other authors are doing. All will have styles of performing in front of an audience that differ to some degree, and you should carefully study these differences. I also take notes at the book events I observe to keep a record I can examine later on about how the authors involved the audience, which types of passages from the book they read, what type of "visuals" they used to present the main subject of the book and the audience's reactions. Consider attending book events by those who write in different genres/areas to get a more comprehensive view of the varying styles of presentation.

XI. Joining Writer Groups

If it is at all possible, join local and regional writer groups. The interaction with other authors can provide a wealth of knowledge. These groups provide a "ready audience" you can use when you would like to try out a draft of a new work. You can discuss and practice new presentations with the other members. You can also discuss ideas for stories with them. The special topics and discussions at meetings can be quite enlightening because you can explore multiple points of view on a full range of subjects in the world of writing. These groups generally discuss everything from the new technologies available to authors to the experiences of promoting their new books. In short, writer groups can be one of the best sources of information—of all types—for you.

There are specific membership requirements, but when you are eligible, also consider applying for membership in The Authors Guild and/or other national author advocacy groups. Membership in such groups will keep you up to date on the latest issues facing the publishing industry. Plus, their regular newsletters and bulletins typically contain articles that provide practical advice in a wide range of areas of interest to those who write. These groups also work to help protect the rights of authors, a worthy mission indeed and one that is deserving of support.

XII. Attending Conferences

Regularly examine the conference schedules for the educational organizations that most closely match the type of writing you do. For instance, the National Council of Teachers of English (NCTE) holds several conferences and meetings each year, and dozens of writers—representing the full range of literature—typically speak at those gatherings. The International Reading Association (IRA) also has meetings several times per year. There are special meetings for those who teach everything from history to science—and everything else in between. These groups are always looking for speakers for their meetings. Consider sending "introduction" letters to the appropriate organizations to let them know you are available to speak—and to let them know the range of presentations you could do for them. Speaking at those conferences is an effective means of promoting your work. Plus, most also have special times built into their meeting schedules during which authors can sell and sign their books. Attending these conferences will provide an opportunity for you to see a large number of other writers, from across the country and at times from across the globe, giving presentations. The knowledge you gain from these conferences will be most helpful as you prepare for your own events.

Concluding thoughts.....

The work authors do *after* book readings, events, and promotions will help complete the cycle essential for achieving the type of successes all writers dream of. It takes dedication and hard work for this dream to come true, but it *does* come true for those who attend to all that should be done before, during, and after events take place. These areas are not static. To the contrary, every book event you do will provide new knowledge that can help shape your future work. Adjustments will be made, and success will be built upon success. Best, the journey along the way to achieving this success will be rewarding and fulfilling.

SECTION 4

Voices from the Road: Authors' Suggestions for Building Successful Book Events

> *"Tell the readers a story! Because without a story, you are merely using words to prove you can string them together in logical sentences."*
> —Anne McCaffrey

In terms of learning to build success with book events, as it is the case with most areas in life, there is nothing like good, old-fashioned experience to provide a positive foundation. However, without at least some general advice and suggestions before venturing in front of an audience, the events can end up being much less than hoped for. As a matter of fact, events can end up absolute disasters.

No two authors are exactly alike when it comes to how they prefer to conduct book readings and events. Some are quite animated when in front of an audience; others are more formal in manner of presentation. Some prefer a great amount of audience involvement; others choose more of a "lecture" type of format and invite only a few questions from those gathered. Still others like the focus of the event to be on the "readings" from selected passages of the book; others prefer to talk more about the "story-behind-the-story" of how the piece came to be written. These differences in styles are wonderful for those who love reading and hearing authors talk about their books. It is precisely *because* of these differences that people keep coming to events. Just as readers anxiously anticipate what will be found inside the covers of a new book, these same readers never know exactly what authors are going to do at the events related to those books—and this helps build the enthusiasm and excitement that keep drawing crowds.

At the same time, even though authors can be quite different in how they approach presenting their work, there are some common threads that run through the most successful book events. I asked for advice and suggestions from authors representing a full range of the types of literature—and event presentation styles. The authors were asked to respond to any or all of eight questions posed to them related to their experiences building and conducting successful book readings and events, with a specific eye toward providing advice and suggestions for new(er) authors. Their responses are presented below in a "Roundtable Advice" format for each question, a structure that should make the information easier for authors to access when building their own book events.

Author Roundtable Advice

> **QUESTION #1: What are the two or three most important pieces of advice for new(er) authors about how to conduct successful book readings and events?**

Brod Bagert:

When doing book events, always remember it's not about *you*. When you sit for an hour and don't autograph a single book; when you present to an audience of three—it's never about you. It's about giving yourself to those who come to hear you and making the event a success for the dedicated person who went out on a limb to bring you there. So open your heart, let the best of you pour out, and be thankful that you don't have to be a banker.

————

Kevin O'Brien:

I truly believe you have to plan your author-event as if you were throwing a terrific party. You need to make sure people show up, and you need to make sure your audience—your guests—have fun.

To get people in the seats, I'll post the event on Facebook and my website at least ten days in advance, and I ask friends to come—and bring friends of theirs, if possible. I'll post another reminder a couple of days prior to the event. Then I cross my fingers and hope people show up. Once they're at the bookstore, I need to make sure they have a good time. That often means entertaining and feeding them—especially if it's a publication party (the first event for that book). Most of the publication parties I've attended lately have had wine and cheese and crackers for the audience. Some authors do even better than that. Maria Semple's *Where'd You Go, Bernadette* publication party at Seattle's Elliott Bay Book Company (a GREAT bookstore, by the way) featured a machine churning out Molly Moons ice cream (a local favorite). My *Tell Me You're Sorry* book release party (also at Elliott Bay Books) was catered by Savior Fork ("Redemption Through Pie"). Guests ate specially-made mini-pies, cheese, crackers, and candy, and they went through ten bottles of wine. At her *Love, Water, Memory* publication party, Jennie Shortridge, had wine and cheese, read from her new book, and sang three songs (including "Every Day I Write the Book"). She was accompanied by her band, "The Rejections," made up of authors from the Seattle 7 Writers group (www.seattle7writers.org) and their spouses. They're pretty damn good, too! They also performed at Carol Cassella's publication party—with songs like "I Want to Be Sedated," and "Girlfriend in a Coma" to salute Carol's medical-based stories. They sang "Psycho Killer" at my *Tell Me You're Sorry* book party, and the crowd went wild. For most publication parties, you don't really need to hire a caterer or a band. But it certainly doesn't hurt!

For a regular book event or author talk, the general rules of drumming up attendance and entertaining your audience still apply. Even at smaller scale signings,

I always have a bowl of Hershey's Minis or Rolos at my signing table, and I always try to be as engaging as possible. Remember, you, the author, are the main attraction at these events, but you're also the host.

———

Chris Crutcher:

These are my best pieces of advice, especially for those who write for younger readers. For one thing, when I visit a school to share my books I consider there are very few students in the audience who want to be writers and even fewer who will. So what's important to me is to let them know what part of my fiction comes out of real life, and why good storytelling focuses on parts of the real world. Almost all my stories are about connectedness, so in my presentations I try to make connection. I don't want to *explain* it—I want to *do* it. So I tell them stories and bring them back to real life. It's important for me to elicit an emotional response from my audience. I want to make them laugh and will do so every chance I get. If I can keep you laughing, I can keep you listening. I also want to make them mad (at humans who do despicable things) and I want to make them cry if I can. In other words, I want my presentation to do the same things I want my books to do. So... I guess, not a lot of explanation and a lot of emotional connection. And I can truthfully say I have very seldom had that not work, and then only when I misread my audience and told the wrong stories.

———

Jimmy Santiago Baca:

Even if you do your very best job of promotion, you can't control the number of people attending your readings. But you *can* read from your chart as if the poem is the world and the world is a small mistake scribbled out on a page you're revising. In short, give them all you've got—your whole effort every time. That is the author's duty and responsibility to an audience.

———

Chris Crowe:

One of the most important things for a successful event is doing all you can to make sure the organization hosting the event is well-prepared. Do they have your books on hand for signing and selling? Have they advertised the event and have you given them the information about you and your book so they can advertise? Have they prepared a clear schedule for what you're expected to do while there? Make sure *all* of these things are taken care of *before* you get to the event.

———

Luis Rodriguez:

One, *prepare*. Pick what you're going to read, marking this in your reading copy if this helps. Have anecdotes, key points, and interesting moments ahead of time. For just about every author, "thinking on your feet" is best done with adequate preparation. Next, however, feel free to get off plan, to be spontaneous, to go with the flow. And third, be real—serious when you need to be, funny when you must. Do not seem forced. Audiences relax when a speaker is relaxed, but know also how to get "on point"—no rambling or going on tangents that have absolutely nothing to do with why you are there.

_____

Mary Ann Hoberman:

Be yourself! At the same time, communicate the love for what you do; some authors forget to share this, and audiences pick up on that. While sharing the work, find in the audience one smiling face and focus on that. Of course, you respond to everyone, but never forget that you are talking to that one smiling face multiplied by the rest of those in the room. This is especially important for those who think they will be nervous in front of crowds. If there are butterflies at first, find that smiling face in the room, and build upon that. When that is done, half the battle is won, and the rest of the event usually goes smoothly from there.

Also don't forget there is a kid in each of us, and you need to tap into that. Trust yourself and have the confidence to tap into your inner child. For those of us who write poetry for children, this also means never talking down to our young readers.

_____

Brad Cook:

First and foremost, make it interesting. The signings and readings I remember most are the ones that were more than an author sitting behind a table. My favorite was a signing complete with actors dressed in Japanese kimono and a samurai, but I've also been to a cocktail hour, tea services, and had wine and cheese in a fancy restaurant where the event was taking place. Be creative —both about what you do and, if possible, the venue where the event is to be held. Never forget that many bookstores will also sponsor events and send representatives to sell books at places other than their bookstores. Explore that as an option if a place is close by that will add greatly to the *atmosphere* for an event.

Second, tell as many people as you can about the event. No one will show if they don't know about it, so post on social media, send out press releases to get on the community calendars, contact writers, tell your friends, and target your readers.

Finally, have reasonable expectations. We all want a line out the door, but the truth is you won't always have a crowd, and that is okay. It happens to the best of us.

——

T.C. Boyle:

My most important piece of advice would be this: carry yourself with fire and exert your charisma. Know that you will blow them away. (This gets easier with experience.)

——

Scott Cawelti:

First, take some visual aids—pictures especially—and laminate them to pass around. These provide an opening focal point; you can explain each photo or illustration then hand it out for individual inspection. This gets the audience engaged quickly, I found.

Second, interact as much as you can. Ask questions about how much they've experienced your topic and in what ways, and use their responses to connect to your specific work. At an event for my last book, which was nonfiction, several audience members usually knew one or more of the family I was writing about, and shared their perceptions, which I compared to my own from my research. This led to a great discussion and a great event.

Last, allow plenty of time for Q and A—this is usually the most memorable and helpful portion of the reading for most attendees.

———

Wendy Marie Hoofnagle:

One word: *emotion*. Because writing can be such a solitary act, authors sometimes forget the live audience that will be attending a reading—and ideally buying the book. Authors can be the best salespeople of their own work: they made their vision a reality, and now they can bring that vision to life. I have seen potentially fascinating stories fall flat because of a lackluster reading, and I have seen mediocre ones made more intriguing with an animated delivery. If public speaking is a daunting prospect, consider taking an acting class—seriously; not only will it make you feel more comfortable being in the spotlight, it will teach you how to breathe life into the words on the page. That can make all the difference in the world at an event.

———

Constance Levy:

Generally speaking, look and sound happy and relaxed—even if you're nervous. Do *not* carry a pile of notes with you; a few cards with prompts should be enough if you need reminders. Wear shoes that are kind to your feet even when standing for extended periods. Trust me—this does make a difference at times. Also, try to visually connect with *all* of your audience as you speak, and if it's a small group get comfortably close to them, not "in your face close" but friendly close, when possible.

———

Jane Henderson:

Above all, enjoy the event. There is nothing more off-putting than an author who seems defensive or resentful or haughty. New authors generally don't, but it can happen. Be thankful for an audience and show your appreciation. Then write thank you notes to organizers. *Don't* forget to do that.

———

Jerome Klinkowitz:

My advice is going to be a little different from what some writers have to say. For me, DO have a reading; do NOT consent to just sitting at a table at or near the store's entry...you will die there, and vow to never write again.

Have friends planted in the audience to stimulate reactions. If you're in a distant city, ask the store to plant at least two clerks in the audience, to feign overwhelming interest and enthusiasm.

Be enthusiastic yourself. After all, you've always wanted to be a writer—so, now, be one.

———

Jennifer Hasheider:

I ask for a media kit when I hire a speaker for Saturday Writers. This usually consists of a .jpg photo of the speaker/author. Please make sure it is a current photo; investing in a professional photo session for media photos will go a very long way and you'll find you have very many uses for professional photos. Also, include a title for your talk and a bit of info about it. Also include a .jpg of your book cover, a brief description, where to buy it—and do not forget your bio. If you are asked to provide these things, it will benefit you to actually send them rather than replying with your website address so the requester must go there and fish for the information they've requested. Perhaps you can prepare a file on your computer so sending this information is an easy click for you.

———

Sally Walker:

Many writers will say this, and I agree, that you should tell as many of your friends and colleagues about the event as you can. Email, telephone calls, note cards, Facebook—use every media form available to you to spread the word.

Also, and this is something that many writers forget to do, contact the local public library in the town where the event will take place (and libraries in towns surrounding it). Let them know about the event—and ask them to help with the publicity.

———

James O'Loughlin:

Never forget that a little humor goes a long way, particularly if your book is on a serious topic. Try to come up with a good "opening" for your talk.

Also, most people retain information better reading than listening, so it is good to prep your listeners for what they are about to hear. Introduce characters or context, in detail if you think necessary (though not spoilers).

One other thing: by the time a book gets published, it may seem like old news to a writer who is probably drafting another project, but stick to your book. Reading from a range of publications (with only a little bit of focus on the new book) conveys to an audience that the book isn't important enough to buy. So, stick mostly to the book you are there to talk about!

———

Nikki Giovanni:

A lot depends upon what you call "success." The fact that people, maybe only a handful, came to hear you is successful. You talk with them about your book and *don't forget* to ask them about themselves. Make the time to get to know those who are there. A large gathering gives less time for asking and more for presenting, but I would always leave time for questions and I would always be happy for whomever came. Focus on those who are there, and don't worry about those who did not come to the event.

———

Delia Ray:

First I need to preface my comments with an admission. I have a love/hate relationship with the public speaking side of our profession. In truth, there have been times I would rather walk across hot coals barefoot than follow through with commitments I've made for book readings or keynote speeches at book festivals and writing conferences. Fortunately, I write novels for middle-grade readers and, most of the time, my audiences are made up of enthusiastic fourth, fifth and sixth graders with a sprinkling of gracious and kind-hearted teachers and librarians thrown in.

But whether I'm addressing an auditorium full of 200 middle-schoolers or 20 teachers at a reading conference breakout session, I always fall back on three trusty habits to help pull me through my natural discomfort with public speaking and bring me to that magical sweet spot where I'm connecting with the crowd and actually embracing and enjoying the process.

1. *Start with humor.* When planning remarks for an event, it can be tempting to overlook or skim over those

first few crucial minutes that we share with an audience. In my early days of public speaking, I would simply plan to thank my sponsor or sponsors, thank the audience for coming, give a little overview of what I was going to be discussing or reading, and bingo! I'd be off and running. Uh...I wish! For me, this approach did nothing to help alleviate that initial period of jitters that I feel with each speaking gig. I've learned that starting with a funny remark or humorous anecdote as an icebreaker, sharing that initial burst of laughter (hopefully!) does wonders to put myself and the audience collectively at ease.

2. *Consider visuals.* I'm a firm believer in using slides to help illustrate my writing and research process. Who doesn't like pictures? Slides not only add variety and clarity to presentations, but they also help to ease the sense that all of the focus will be on YOU and only YOU during your talk. Many of us are conditioned to think that there isn't room for any sort of visual presentation during a traditional book reading. I've found that the typical one-hour format offers plenty of time for slides and that bookstore staff members are very excited about the idea of incorporating this element into the discussion time, as long as I bring my own projector, screen, and computer set-up if necessary.

3. *Practice, but not too much.* When preparing for the release of a new book and upcoming speaking events, I've often typed out my planned talk on my computer. This rather tedious practice has worked well in helping me to organize my thoughts. But I've learned that

my presentation changes by leaps and bounds once I practice my written speech for a select few family members, friends, or colleagues. One or two small practice sessions will quickly reveal the awkward or languishing spots or points where smoother transitions and clearer explanations are needed. That said, I avoid practicing too much so that my presentation feels fresh and new during my first rounds of giving it.

———

Rob Rains:

One truth is that marketing is more important than the quality of the book. Merely writing a great book and hoping that is enough to generate sales is unrealistic. The books that are on *The New York Times* bestseller list are there because they have the best marketing plans behind them.

Marketing of the book can be done in multiple ways, and the authors who become the most involved through Twitter, Facebook, other social media and reviews on internet sales sites are key. Try to identify a target audience for your book and heavily market the book to that audience. Also, never forget word of mouth still is one of the best sales techniques around.

One example which worked well for me was for my book *Intentional Walk,* about the Christian faith of the St. Louis Cardinals. We scheduled a book signing at a Barnes and Noble. The store printed out flyers and distributed them to multiple churches in the area, and this helped us generate a good crowd.

———

Mel Glenn:

The prime directive is so simple I am almost ashamed to reveal it: Be yourself, your natural, charming, hopefully humorous self. (This is especially important when dealing with kids.) Don't lecture, don't read. Don't wait for questions at the end. I want kids to interrupt me at any time. There isn't a question I haven't heard, including, "Mr. Glenn, you're old, you're bald, how can you write for kids?" I live for such moments of spontaneity. Don't drone—be enthusiastic. As a teacher and a presenter, your presentation is performance art. Don't be afraid to be "theatrical." And above all (!), never wing it. Always, always come prepared.

———

Lee Bennett Hopkins:

My advice for others would be exactly what I always tell myself before a book event. First, be prepared; make the time to be wonderful. Second, talk slowly; the presentation is *not* a race. Finally, relax, have a good time, and always use eye contact with an audience. If these are attended to, events, over time, become wonderful experiences for writers.

———

J. Patrick Lewis:

The most important thing to remember is that your audience did not come to be educated but to be

entertained. That doesn't mean that your poetry reading must replicate a stand-up comic's routine. But try
to avoid choosing the most recondite of your poems to
read. This is tantamount to shooting tranquilizing darts
at your audience. However, I confess that I was once
quite charmed when a listener asked me if I was going
to be on Comedy Central anytime soon.

Next, set a time limit for yourself of no more than a
half hour, at least for a poetry reading. There is no worse
sin than maundering on *ad nauseum* until your guests'
eyes have glazed over or they are scrambling for the
exits. After you have shared your poetry (or other work),
it is then time to involve the audience as much as possible. If those in the audience don't ask you questions,
then ask them questions. Many writers forget this is a
valuable technique for getting a good discussion going.

———

Robert James Waller:

Know thyself. If public speaking bothers you, get over it
by practice and preparation. Also, if a truly annoying or
sensitive question is asked during an event, invite the
person to speak to you for a moment after everything
else is completed; that usually takes care of that situation. Authors should also be prepared for this: hang-
ers-on who want an extended dialogue as you prepare
to leave; tell them you have a tight schedule and politely
extricate yourself. Note that an alert bookstore person
should help you by taking your arm and aiding your
getaway.

I hate to say it, and I'm not trying to scare anyone, but now and then there are real crazies out there, especially in large cities. I have done some programs with armed guards standing nearby. Everything depends on the sophistication of the audience and the nature of the book. You can usually gauge this by attire and by making use of an informal pre-program discussion.

I write both economics books and novels. For the economics books I provide a précis, an overview of the book, in straightforward prose, since the typical audience does not want to hear about my brilliant integral calculus equations concerning human discount functions. The worst approach is an author gripping the podium, head down, and droning through his/her masterpiece for a half-hour. Be relaxed, you are in control. Study oral interpretation, if you have trouble with public speaking and reading prose in an interesting fashion.

Also, be careful of reporters in attendance, if your book is controversial. They always have an agenda. Never forget that. At the same time, don't give out your email address or phone number. Give out your mailing address if you must and you'll likely never hear from the person who wants to waste more of your time.

The age-old question about getting published frequently arises at book events. Refer people to the Internet to find names of agents, warning them about the large number of shysters who offer to read your book for a fee. Refer them to the latest edition of *Writers Market*. Don't give out the name of your agent without permission.

Finally, send follow-up notes to the bookstore manager, expressing your appreciation for hosting your event.

———

Jeremy Schraffenberger:

Since I'm primarily a poet, I have something of an advantage over my prose counterparts when I give a reading because if one of my poems falls flat, well, I've always got the next one coming up. Ordering these poems is for me, then, the most important part of the reading. Even if only subtly, the ordering of poems can offer something of a narrative arc, making the reading feel more cohesive than if I simply read what I considered to be my "best" material regardless of theme or style. I'd say the same advice is important for those who might be reading prose selections from multiple books.

I feel like I've learned a lot about what to do—and what not to do—in a reading by attending hundreds of readings over the years. So I'd suggest that new writers go to every reading they possibly can. By seeing other people read, you can really get a sense of what your most natural style might be when it's your turn behind the lectern.

———

Arnold Adoff:

Based upon my experiences and what I really believe in, here goes. Whether the author will be speaking to a school, a library, or a reading group of some type, it is always best to visit with those in charge before the event to find out exactly what they would like to see happen at the event. Too often this isn't communicated effectively, and the event that takes place isn't at all what had been advertised for that day—and that's a terrible thing.

In addition, when visiting schools and similar groups, make sure it is specified how many sessions will be done. I've gone to schools and found out I was, much to my surprise, expected to do seven or eight presentations! It can be really crazy.

Also, and I can't emphasize this enough, make all the necessary arrangements before the event to make sure copies of your book will be there. I've known too many authors who weren't involved enough in this area, and they found themselves with nothing to sell, which is a horrible experience to go through and is also very embarrassing.

QUESTION #2: *What do you do to prepare for book readings and events?*

Jerome Klinkowitz:

When preparing for events, look through your book to find an interesting but also self-contained passage that can stand alone without a lot of contextual explanation when you read it to an audience. Novelist Meg Wolitzer says that usually a book's beginning will work this way. At the same time, be aware of time limits: gauge how many pages you think you can read in twenty minutes, and then cut that number of pages in half.

———

Luis Rodriguez:

I've done hundreds of readings over two decades so I have stories, points, moments in my head. I have poems and passages I've read often. Now at book events and readings I'm ready, to the point I can read from or discuss things I'd never done before. The main thing is for me to be interested and engaged—never take any audience for granted and always give my best no matter how many people show up or what the venue is. *That* is what I would recommend to others. This will all come with time, so be patient.

———

Scott Cawelti:

Usually I go over the main points and the supporting quotes from the book, and make sure I can find them easily on the fly. I use post-it notes that stick up, labeled. Don't embarrass yourself by not being able to readily find passages you want to read. I've seen this happen to many authors, and it is not a pretty sight to see.

———

Arnold Adoff:

Before I go to book events, I make notes, mostly about sequence. That is, I write down the "areas" I want to cover and in the specific order. I do this so I can keep myself on track and, if discussion gets us off into another area, I can just look at my notes, find out where we were, and go on from there.

I think about what I want to wear. My clothes represent me and who I am. I wear a lot of black, which has become something of a trademark for me. I'm comfortable in that, and so I'm comfortable at the events. Style and externalities are always important to me. If an author is comfortable with it, wear five more bracelets. Wear lots of chains around the neck or many scarves. Wear a large and interesting hat—anything to show an author can be freaky and distinctive and yet just an ordinary person. It's always fun to poke holes in conventionality.

———

Constance Levy:

I always over-prepare because the same plan won't work for all events, at least not for me. At the same time, I try to be flexible and fit my activities to the group. It's helpful to find out as much as possible about the nature of the event, the expected audience size, and my place in it. Sometimes it's necessary to adapt to the unexpected so I can shift gears on the spot. That may mean choosing different examples to read and use for discussion, so it is always good to have "back-up" passages just in case. I'd recommend this for all authors.

Also—and this is important—if it's a bookstore or library reading and I haven't rounded up friends and family to pad attendance and the host group hasn't publicized, I prepare myself to expect few if any (yes, that happens) in attendance. Once I had an attendance of one, a teacher. We had a lovely hour together talking about poetry and how to bring it to her students. I think she appreciated it, at least. Always have something up your sleeve in case the unexpected shows up.

———

Jennifer Hasheider:

Get the word out about your talk (and book, of course) as much as possible long *before* the day of the event. Many writers forget that doing this may lead to more speaking engagements because of all the publicity and hype.

Also, make arrangements in advance to have someone take photographs of you during the event that you can use on your website.

Another thing: You may even be paid for your talk. If your goal is selling books and telling folks about your book—and if you are being paid—avoid charging high amounts for your appearance. Always remember the pool is large and you may not be chosen by a nonprofit organization if money becomes a huge factor. Finally, don't be afraid to ask for hotel or fuel expenses if you travel very far—but ask for this well in advance of the visit and *not* the day of. Some authors ask for this the day of, and that is just wrong.

———

Brad Cook:

Practice, Practice, Practice. I always go over what I am going to say or read before the event so many times I can practically do it all in my sleep. This may seem like over-kill, but it will pay dividends when in front of audiences.

———

T. C. Boyle:

I sleep, eat, brush my teeth. Of course, if this is the first event of a tour, I will prepare by performing my story aloud to my long-suffering friends and family, just to hear its rhythms. They will be honest with you in ways others wouldn't dare.

———

Sally Walker:

I choose several of the most important points about the book that I want to bring to the audience's attention. Usually I include a couple of research anecdotes. For nonfiction, if you can hold a short PowerPoint that shows examples of research materials, that's really great. Audiences *love* the visuals, and not enough authors try incorporating them.

———

James O'Loughlin:

My advice for preparation? Read your material out loud to yourself at least once. Use a pen or highlighter to note areas when you need to place a particular emphasis on a word. I tend to use different voices for dialogue, but I know that's not everyone's thing. Basically, a reading is a performance, and it should be prepared for much as an actor prepares for a staged reading. New readers have a tendency to race through their material too quickly. Slow down and enjoy yourself. If you do, the audience will enjoy the event as well.

———

Jimmy Santiago Baca:

I challenge myself to try to give my best and always to respect the poetry. If I do that, I know the rest will be taken care of by the energy and magic of the language.

———

Nikki Giovanni:

You know your book so I guess you'd shower, leave your bad attitude at home, and come to enjoy your audience. The emphasis here is to prepare to have a positive experience—for yourself and those who come to listen to you.

———

Lee Bennett Hopkins:

I prepare notes on an index card—and I recommend this for everyone else as well, and especially for new authors. A few brief words makes me aware of what NOT to forget to say or read, which can happen in the excitement of the moment.

———

QUESTION #3: *How do you involve the audience in your readings and events?*

Jerome Klinkowitz:

At all times show more interest in them than in yourself or your own work. On the other hand, don't read anything without prefacing it with a brief, engaging anecdote, one that will let them share your experience. Try to make involvement more of a continuing dialogue than a formal question and answer format. Always be aware of your listeners; when you've read something you particularly like, pause, look up, and say, "That's pretty good, isn't it?" This always worked for James Dickey. Don't be afraid to gently tease your audience; Kurt Vonnegut did, and was loved.

———

Kevin O'Brien:

As much as possible, I involve the audience in my author events. I will point out other authors in the crowd and ask them to stand—while I plug their books. It's great for the authors—as well as their fans in attendance. If someone in the audience is in my Acknowledgments, I'll give them a shout out and explain how they contributed to the book (it helps if you can tell amusing/entertaining stories about them). Not only is this a nice way to thank people, it also keeps things lively and makes the presentation more engaging for everybody.

———

Jimmy Santiago Baca:

I'm not much on involving the audience in my poems, but I've had some readings with an opportunity for the audience to ask questions. But involving the audience, no, it seems more an exercise in seeking attention and approval and poets don't need either to be good poets. However, that's just me. Others may feel differently.

———

Luis Rodriguez:

I really pay attention to the audience. For example, I acknowledge friends or people I know in the audience right at the very beginning. I try to pick questions from around the room so that all sections of the group get involved. Many authors forget to do this, and many people don't get involved who'd like to be. As much as I can I bring into the discussion those from both genders, all races in the room, etc. I also love Q&A—some of my best comments come from these. I never back away from any challenge, but I also never take anyone's dignity away. I try not to get emotionally carried away, but I'm open to tears or healthy doses of anger if this is proper and comes naturally.

———

Nancy White Carlstrom:

Of course, most of my experiences have been with younger readers, so my advice falls into that area. I think participation is key in presenting to very young and even not-so-very young children. I take show and tell pieces with me such as a small baby outfit with a bear face on the front, suggesting it may have given me the idea for the "face on the seat" of the pj's in *Jesse Bear, What Will You Wear?*—"My pj's with feet and face on the seat, that's what I'll wear tonight." The show and tell pieces help connect everything so well.

I also take bits and pieces of the whole picture book process, sample of a rough draft, galley sheet, illustrators' dummy, f & g (folded and gathered pages unbound).

I take a large uncut press sheet showing one of my picture books, all thirty-two pages plus covers on one page. Sometimes, if the presentation is local, I take in an original painting from my office wall that is an illustration from a book. And it's always fun to bring along *Swim The Silver Sea, Joshie Otter* in Japanese or *Northern Lullaby* in Korean. Also, because many of my books are set in Alaska I take something from Alaska, usually a set of four dog booties, or dog socks as I call them, and have the youngest ones try to guess what they are for, which becomes a fun game.

In reading aloud from my books, I will often have students join in on the refrains or leave out words for them to fill in. The key to a successful presentation for a very young audience is to blend as many ways of getting them involved as possible. At the same time, I think about the pacing of my program in the same way I think about the pacing of a picture book.

———

Jeremy Schraffenberger:

I think we have to admit that some readings can be just deadly dull, so any kind of levity that can be injected into the event is welcome. This could be as simple as telling a joke or humorous anecdote, of course, but you can also be more creative. For example, at a reading I attended by the novelist Kate Christensen, she read brief passages from four of her previous books, telling the audience that the first person who guessed the unifying theme of these selections would get a free copy of her latest book. The atmosphere in the room was different from other readings I've attended—lighter and a little giddy—and what's more, this little contest seemed to make the audience listen more carefully than they otherwise might have.

———

Brad Cook:

Anything you can do to engage the audience is important. Q&A's are usually a good way to start, but include the audience in your readings by having them play the parts, especially when dialogue is involved between/among characters. Many authors are hesitant to try this, but it can be a great deal of fun for everyone and bring the work to life in a very special way. Bring multiple copies of your book and mark or number specific passages to be read by each voice. Then, assign to some in the audience the different passages to read aloud. Even if they don't read the passages well, the audience still loves this—and it also helps set a nice tone for the rest of the event.

———

T.C. Boyle:

First I put them at ease with spontaneous remarks, then I perform for them—lights out, everybody seated—and then take questions. If done well, this is enough for me.

———

Scott Cawelti:

I've always believed that Q and A gets everyone involved in a memorable way. Always leave plenty of time—up to half of your presentation—for questions, and raise your own if no one raises their hand immediately. Almost always, several people will raise questions about your research methods, your writing processes, your next project, etc. At the same time, try to think of the questions that people will ask, and then practice your answers. That is an effective technique.

———

Constance Levy:

In a large group I try to bring the listeners into my world by telling a story or two about how a particular poem came about or the saga of getting that first book published. But I do find that questions following a presentation are a great way to involve the audience and often a lot of fun. Many will be shy about asking questions, so don't forget to give ample time for those individuals to raise hands and get involved. Too often authors don't get questions right away and cut off the event early. Wait for the questions!

———

Jennifer Hasheider:

This may seem like a small thing, but it is NOT. If a "Question and Answer" session is given during your talk, be sure to repeat the question that is asked of you before you answer it. This is especially important in a large group. Few things damage the potential for excellent discussion and interaction than people not being able to hear what others are saying. Always repeat the questions.

———

James O'Loughlin:

There is a lot of possibility for using social media to prepare an audience for a reading. Is there any way to draw from an audience's personal experience to relate to the topic? Sometimes just asking a question of the audience helps to engage people. Establishing those kind of connections are what make for memorable readings.

———

Nikki Giovanni:

You are talking with intelligent people. Treat them with respect. Period. Always remember that when you are with an audience.

———

Lee Bennett Hopkins:

Personally, I love Q/A. So many different avenues open up. You might get questions that will take you to places you never even thought of before, so encourage everyone to ask any questions they'd like, either about the story or your work as a writer. Many are fascinated by the process a writer goes through while creating a book, and questions related to that can bounce back to more discussion about the book at hand.

_____

QUESTION #4: *What do you do during readings and events that help make them successful?*

Grant Tracey:

Presenters need to remember that the audience can't see what's on the page as you're reading your work. On the page, readers can see that new paragraph starts often signal when dialogue is switching up. This formatting, like shot/reverse shot compositions in film, allows readers to see and sense that the focus of interest, the person speaking, has changed. For writers, these paragraph breaks allow us to avoid unnecessary dialogue tags, like "he said, she said." However, when reading those dialogue tags become necessary because the audience can't see those paragraph shifts, so your presenting copy should probably be different from your published or reading copy. Include more dialogue tags for the presenting copy as opposed to the on-the-page reader's copy, and this will make the readings *much more* enjoyable for audiences.

_____

Jimmy Santiago Baca:

Read slow. Let the words float out and do their work in peoples hearts. And don't take yourself so seriously. Be lighthearted even when referencing a crisis (something happening around the world), and for god's sake—keep the academic posturing to a minimum. Eliminate the "how important I am" bullsh@$—be one with the community, be one with the audience, be one with life's hardships. We've had enough cuteness, enough nerd-attraction, enough of the mystery of poets.

———

Nancy White Carlstrom:

I always try to personally extend grace and kindness to each child and adult, especially as they ask questions and also afterwards, to students who might be shy about speaking up in a group but who clearly want to talk with me. I should add that patience helps, too.

———

Brad Cook:

I like to interject some humor, not so much it's like a comedy act, but making the audience laugh, or at least chuckle, will help keep them interested. Tell them something about your travel to the event or about something that recently happened to you (or another writer you know) while doing another book event. Basically, humor unifies people, so anything that you can share that will make them laugh will go a long way toward establishing rapport with the audience.

———

Rob Rains:

People like celebrities. If you can align your book with a celebrity, whether it is to make an endorsement or write the foreword, and then get them to come to a book signing/appearance with you, you will draw a much bigger crowd. For example, Hall of Famer Stan Musial did a foreword for a book I wrote several years ago. I got him to come to a book signing with me, and people were lined up outside the door. They didn't care about the book—they were buying it to get Stan Musial's autograph. One possibility if the celebrity won't come to a signing is to get him to sign books in private and take them with you. It won't be personalized, but they will still get the autograph. This isn't possible with every book, but when possible, I highly recommend it.

———

T.C. Boyle:

Many forget the importance of lighting, which can make or break some events. In bookstores, this isn't as easy to manage but, if possible, the lights must be down. The audience always responds better in the dark—they feel anonymous and free. Once they feel this freedom, the questions flow and the discussion can become incredibly good.

———

Jennifer Hasheider:

Many times our speakers for Saturday Writers read from their books during their talks. Even though the book is your work, and you've rewritten it 520 times—there is no guarantee you will be any good reading any of it aloud. No one likes to hear monotone reading, and this will do nothing to entice the group to buy your book. If you sound boring reading it, then folks may view it as a boring book.

1. Choose the portion(s) of the book to read aloud carefully. Be sure it pertains to the topic you wish to emphasize. If the group is interested in your main topic, don't read a passage that has nothing to do with it. Keep their attention, and give enough "backstory" to catch them up before you begin reading, but don't give away too much plot.

2. Know the venue where you are reading. Consider if you should read questionable content or profanity verbatim. Many don't think about this, and terrible things can result.

3. Before the meeting, rehearse! Read your work out loud, read it in front of a mirror. Be sure you read clearly, with expression and inflection. Use your hands, make faces, use voices, and move around. Be entertaining. If the audience sees you are enjoying reading your book, they'll want to read it for enjoyment also.

4. If you are using a microphone, try to stay on it and be sure to make eye contact (throughout your entire talk, really). Many wander away from the microphone and forget or don't realize they can no longer be heard. Oops!

Be confident and proud of your work. If you are proud of your book, then we will believe it must be a masterpiece and want to buy it.

———

Robert James Waller:

I arrive early and chat with people as they filter in, sometimes to the mild discomfort of the bookstore manager, since it is slightly unusual. This approach is somewhat different from the typical "introduce author—author does lecture or reading—Q&A follows." The informal chatting lets the attendees get to know the author ahead of the formalities and provides the author information about the audience. You might ask where people are from or how the local sports team is doing or the condition of the arts in their town or just talk about the weather. If a question pertinent to your book or a more general one about writing arises, make a note of it and promise to address it in the Q&A.

———

Sally Walker:

Be friendly and welcoming. Let the audience know you appreciate them coming. Be willing to let the audience members share short, pertinent experiences related to something in your book, along the line of personal insights.

———

James O'Loughlin:

As a host for book readings and events, I like to have coffee or food available and some music playing before things get started, but many times a host (or an author) won't have control over those things. because of the venue. Still, setting a relaxed tone that allows people to enjoy themselves is my first priority and can make a huge difference.

_____

Nikki Giovanni:

I let any audience know I am glad to be there and glad to see them. Many writers forget to say this, but it's important to do. This can get an event off to a very good start.

_____

J. Patrick Lewis:

To loosen things up a bit, I first find my cell phone and ask my audience if I can take a picture of them. Two reasons: a) for posterity, and b) I tell them I have to provide my wife with proof that I was here! That usually sets a lighter tone for the evening. Try this—or think of something similar to make that initial positive connection with the audience.

_____

Jeremy Schraffenberger:

One thing I do at almost all of my readings where I'm selling my books myself (as opposed to being at a bookstore where they will do the selling) is give a discount on my books. If the list price is \$16.95, I'll round down to \$15. Sometimes this isn't possible if other people are handling the books and money for you, but if you're traveling with your own copies, a small discount will help sell more copies of your books—and making change is much easier, too!

———

Arnold Adoff:

If I'm going to a school to share my books, which many authors do, I always try to get the art teacher—sometimes also the music teacher—involved so they can get the students involved through some type of contest before my visit. I especially like to have the students all do bookmarks. After the bookmarks are made, I ask that they be sent to me before I go there, and I autograph them and send them back so that every kid has an autograph. There usually isn't time for autographs when going from group to group, but if this is done in advance, they all end up with a keepsake for the event, which makes them very happy. Through this, no kid is deprived. Not all will be able to purchase a book, but this way they all get something, and that is very important.

At the same time, and this is a frightening prospect for some authors who go to schools, stick around and have lunch with the students. I try to do this without the teachers present because the kids will behave very differently with me and will open up in special ways when their teachers are not around. I've had some of my best book discussions while having pizza with students in the school cafeteria. Don't be afraid to try this. This can be a great and memorable experience.

I also like to begin each session with who I am and give personal anecdotes of myself and my life. Not all authors feel comfortable doing this, but this sharing really helps me establish a connection with the audience. I suggest all authors at least experiment with this to see how it works for them.

———

Jerome Klinkowitz:

A ploy for success: Wear a t-shirt or sweatshirt that has a town or school logo on it. Several in the audience are bound to react to it ("Hey, you were at Marquette! Did you know so-and-so?"). Lie and say you did.

———

Luis Rodriguez:

Be on time and never talk or read too much. A good maxim is "leave them wanting more"—but don't leave huge gaps either.

———

Scott Cawelti:

Visual aids. Visual aids. Visual aids. Enough said.

———

QUESTION #5: *How should authors balance reading from the book and interacting with the audience during events?*

Chris Crowe:

More than 60 minutes, even with an engaged adult audience, is too long. Plan for something under an hour, with a 60-40 or 70-30 ration of reading to questions. Older audiences can manage longer readings. Younger audiences need questions and perhaps some sort of presentation to hold their attention.

———

Luis Rodriguez:

Be cognizant of audience interest and reactions. A good guide, at least for me, is to read more than talk. Most poems or prose passages don't require much explaining—they should largely stand on their own. But expertly weaving talk with a reading can be compelling. Some of the most interesting aspects in public readings are the talk around a poem or passage—again the stories, color, facts. Have purpose behind such talk. If you can, and are good at this, have a funny story or line. Humor glues any audience with a speaker.

———

Brad Cook:

Unless you are going to do a dramatic reading, I'd suggest keeping the reading to less than twenty minutes. There is nothing worse than putting an audience to sleep, which most of us have done at one time or another.

_____

Jane Henderson:

Especially if it's a large audience, don't read too long. Those in the back may have trouble hearing. I actually think 10 minutes of reading is about right. Perhaps even do two or three short readings, with quick explanatory set ups, if the book lends itself to that format. Readers want to hear about you and your stories, about your inspirations, etc. They also like to be entertained. A humorous anecdote is often effective. As for Q&As, if the audience is eagerly asking questions, then I'd continue answering until people seem to be getting restless. If it's a small audience and no one raises a hand, offer a bit of information about your background and see if that generates some questions.

_____

T.C. Boyle:

It depends on the author. Many do not like to perform. Many cannot. In these cases, perhaps an onstage interview will work better. Personally, I believe in the power of story, and that two-thirds of any show I give is just that: a show. It is the fiction that carries the night.

_____

James O'Loughlin:

I'm not sure there are hard and fast rules about this, but in general the reading should take more time than the discussion. It is good to have a little something extra in reserve, just in case your main reading doesn't take as long as you anticipated. Also, it is good to have some banter ready to go at the beginning of a Q&A. In my experience, it often takes people a little while to formulate questions, so don't let an awkward silence throw you off.

_____

Constance Levy:

This is what I learned from a second grader a long time ago. These are his exact words: "Don't talk; just read the poems." For me, that means it depends on the group and what they came to hear. You can't go wrong by alternating talking and reading to keep it lively.

_____

Sally Walker:

Reading about three to four pages is good if the work is fiction. More than five pages gets tedious. If it's nonfiction, the audience really wants to hear research adventures and insights. But if you have a riveting short section to read aloud, by all means do so.

_____

Nikki Giovanni:

Let's not forget the purpose of the reading is to do something to encourage the audience members to want the book. You read some from the book but it's also good if you talk about something not in the book which helped you get to another stage. In other words, involve your audience every way you can to make the book, and the event, interesting for all.

———

Mel Glenn:

Even in the best readings, it's often a one-way conversation. After a while, people, and especially kids, drift off. It is necessary to involve them. Whatever length of time I have, I always divide it in half. The first half I entertain; the second half I say, "Now it's your turn." I have many, many prompts and exercises that will get kids to write and share with the assembled group. For example, a writing prompt might be, "The Bruges are coming. The Bruges are coming." What is a Bruge? Answer: anything you want it to be. And this gets the discussion fired up and helps balance the presentation.

———

Lee Bennett Hopkins:

If one is reading poetry, keep it short, perhaps three or four poems. If it is a chapter from a book, choose a short one or excerpt it. You must, however, preface the piece to put it into context. Too many don't do this, which leads to a lot of blank faces. Make the time to do the proper "set up" for the passages read. This helps create a nice balance in events. Also, speak like an actor when appropriate. Always read slowly. And, don't forget: It is not easy for groups to listen for too long.

———

Robert James Waller:

That depends on the venue and the author's comfort level with Q&A. In most circumstances, I use about a 50-50 split totaling forty minutes in all and tend to enjoy the Q&A segment. This leaves a few minutes at the end for those who want to talk privately.

Moreover, I don't always read from the book, but rather present a truncated lecture on writing and the arts in general, which I illustrate by reading short passages from the book as I proceed.

———

Jimmy Santiago Baca:

I like reading for reading's sake—just read. Then later have a discussion from the reading. Thirty to forty-five minutes for reading—likewise for discussion. Then the book signing, dinner, and fly home. This works for me.

———

Jerome Klinkowitz:

In terms of reading/discussion, a 50-50 balance works well for me. Interpolated, not segmented.

———

Scott Cawelti:

Leave about 20 minutes minimum for audience responses, or pause during your presentation if anyone raises questions during your talk. The more audience interaction the better, in my experience.

———

QUESTION #6: *What are the pitfalls new(er) authors should try to avoid while conducting readings and events?*

Brad Cook:

I can't emphasize this enough—Don't step on your own toes by holding too many signings too close together. Spread your events across the city, and don't hold them all in one week. The temptation, especially right after a book comes out, is to see how many events can be scheduled immediately. This usually results in a disaster because too many events will result in small audiences—or no audiences in some cases!

Kevin O'Brien:

I'm terrible at reading out loud, so at my book events, I just get up there and tell stories and interact with the audience. No one seems to mind too much.

I have to admit, I've never heard one person say after a reading (and I've been to scores of them), "Gee, I wish they'd read more from the book..." Unless an author is an excellent reader or has a background in performing arts, the "reading" portion of a book event can get pretty old pretty fast. It's ideal when the author reads from the book two times during the presentation—with segments around seven or eight minutes apiece, and off-the-cuff remarks between them. Better to leave the audience wanting more!

Luis Rodriguez:

Don't be wary of nerves. To this day I get nervous. I use this to keep energized. But nerves can be distracting if you don't find the confidence in your story and writings. Own your stories, your expressions, your verse. Feel comfortable in the skin of what you've written or experienced.

————

Delia Ray:

Reading too long! The reading portion of an author appearance should be treated as a teaser, and that authors should limit their readings to 15 minutes, 20 at the most. In my experience, readers come to these events hungry to get to know the author on a more personal level—where we get our ideas, and how we went about creating the book. These events should offer attendees an exclusive glimpse into the author's world, far beyond what they could perceive if they simply opened our books and read a couple of chapters on their own, or read an article or review online. To me, the best recipe for a successful author event, piquing curiosity, and selling more books, is to spend most of my allotted time sharing the most fascinating experiences and discoveries I encountered during the course of writing my latest book. In other words, the reading is merely the icing on top of the cake, not the main layer of my presentation.

————

Arnold Adoff:

I'm going to tell a story on myself—as a cautionary tale. I did a book event at Wright State a number of years ago and didn't realize the clock in the cafeteria was busted. I must have talked about two hours before I took a breath or let anyone else have a chance to speak. Time management—and having a plan for each session is a must. Otherwise, you can fall in love with the sound of your own voice and get lost in your own little world—and the event becomes unbearable for everyone but yourself!

A very important consideration: If a payment or some type of honorarium is involved with an appearance, get everything in writing in advance—the contract and agreement. I've been stiffed a few times in the past, so I want others to know that can happen unless everything is taken care of up front. I mention this here because many authors go to great expense to get materials and supplies for events, and if the payment does not come through, the author is left to take a financial hit.

———

T.C. Boyle:

It depends on the material. If it is a short story, lay it on them. Let's distinguish between the art and the academic. Explanations are not necessary at a reading. Fire is. Too many authors forget that.

———

Scott Cawelti:

Offering nothing more than a lecture with a few passages

from your work will put your audience to sleep. The idea is to engage your audiences as much as possible with your ideas and prose—so they want to hear and read more.

———

Constance Levy:

As a new author, you may be tempted to try to pour out everything you have planned and rush to include all the wonderful material you have ready. Pace yourself and give the best parts all the time they need. Save the rest for the next talk.

———

Sally Walker:

Don't just read from your book!!! The audience can read the book for themselves. They came to see and hear YOU. Share of yourself and the writing and/or research process.

———

Jerome Klinkowitz:

Pitfalls: You are facing an audience of strangers (as Vonnegut always cautioned); your first job is to convince them that you are a trustworthy and likable person. Would they buy a used car from you? You are a sales-person for your book, something that should never be forgotten.

———

James O'Loughlin:

It's hard to insist that readers be relaxed, but be relaxed! Nervous readers read too fast and without modulation. Audiences like it when someone enjoys being on stage, and they pick up on that quickly.

———

Nikki Giovanni:

Avoid arrogance. Enough said.

———

Lee Bennett Hopkins:

If you are well prepared you shouldn't have any trouble. Do not "wing it," as so many seem to do these days. Sloppy presentations leave a bad impression—and few book sales.

———

Jimmy Santiago Baca:

I may be in my own world here, but here are my thoughts on this. Don't be cool. Don't be a career-climber at readings. Don't network at events. Don't kiss-ass. Don't be agreeable for the sake of being invited other places. Don't sacrifice your honor by seeking awards or accolades or distinctions or winning contests. Be real and read your own work from the list of items you prepared for the reading. Be true to yourself. Children, adults, the world needs truth. Truth is a rare endangered creature these days.

———

QUESTION #7: *Any additional advice/suggestions for new(er) authors?*

Jennifer Hasheider:

Finding a speaking gig for a group such as ours (Saturday Writers) is a terrific way to get the word out for a new book. Our group usually has 40-50 attendees per meeting. We generally hire our speakers to talk about a specific writing topic. As an author, you've likely rewritten your work numerous times. This means you can prepare a very good talk about your editing technique (for example), using various passages from your new book in your lesson. You may not feel like an expert on any particular writing topic, but getting your book published gave you a ton of experience. You know more than you think and writers are always interested in learning from those who have gone before us. Writers groups are a perfect place for authors to hone their skills in terms of presentation style.

———

Kevin O'Brien:

Any author can tell you, some book signing sessions are utter hell. You never know how many people will show up to a signing—and neither does the hosting bookstores. I had a signing years ago, where they'd set up forty chairs in front of my podium. Only one of those chairs was occupied—by some poor customer reading a self-help book. The store clerk told me, "If he's not here to see you, I'll ask him to sit somewhere else."

"Who exactly would he be making room for?" I asked. Mr. Self-Help and the store clerk were the only ones who sat through my brief, very brief talk. In poorly attended signings like this one, the clerk always tries to take the blame. "You know, Tuesday nights can be awfully slow," or "We shouldn't have scheduled you opposite Pancake Dinner Night at the high school," or even bold face lies like, "We had Justin Bieber in here last week, and hardly anybody showed up." Then the clerk asked me to sign a book for him, which was really nice—despite it being an obvious pity purchase.

After that particular signing, I started telling stores in advance that most of the time I wouldn't be lecturing or reading from my book. But I'd be happy to sit at a desk strategically located in the store—with copies of my books. That way, I could smile at people as they passed, interact—and push my thrillers. This worked pretty well, especially after I put a dish full of mini-Hershey bars out with the books. I started that trick around the time I had my first *New York Times* bestseller, *The Last Victim*. Just a coincidence? I think not!

But even then, I've had slow sessions when no one will stop by my table. The time drags on, the frozen smile on my face begins to hurt, and I start eating up my own chocolates. But then someone approaches me, and I'm so, so hopeful—until they ask: "Where's the Social Studies Section?" "It's probably with my will to live," I want to answer. "I have no clue where that is either."

But the truth is that every bookstore signing is a great opportunity to meet the people who work in the stores—selling my books. There are times when I've met readers who made a special trip to see me. And I've received emails from people who got hooked on my thrillers after meeting me at a signing.

As my thrillers have become more popular, the signings have become easier—and even fun. And yes, I'll do talks and lectures now.

(Note: Excerpt from Kevin O'Brien's essay, "Notes from Book Event Hell.")

––––––

Rob Rains:

Look for non-traditional places to hold a book signing. They all don't have to be at a bookstore. Try to schedule appearances where there will be a natural audience—speeches to business groups if it is a business book, a group of fans if it is a baseball book, etc. Also try to work these appearances around the major book-buying holidays—Christmas, Mother's Day, and Father's Day. Another reality which hasn't changed is that more people still buy books to give as gifts to other people than buy for themselves. That's one of the big reasons why the holidays are so important for authors.

––––––

Jimmy Santiago Baca:

Don't let day-to-day readings interfere with your solitude as a poet. If you left it up to these reading-agents and speaker's businesses, the poet would only be out there day and night blabbing away. Get the hell away from the touring and public bullsh@$ and get your ass to a refuge where only silence accompanies your solitary travels into the imagination. Stop seeking fame and money and read, read, read, and then write.

_____

Chris Crowe:

If you plan to use an LCD projector and aren't bringing one yourself, make sure you ask if they will have one on hand—along with a tech person in case something goes wrong. The tech person is vital because you won't have time to mess with the equipment. Also, if the event is at a school, have the students been prepared for your visit? Have they read your book? Make sure they have before you go there. If you're going to do a Q&A, have the questions been prepared and reviewed in advance? You must do this.

_____

Mary Ann Hoberman:

Many new authors are nervous about standing in front of audiences. Just remember that the more you do this, the more confident you will become. Over the years I've also discovered authors should take the measure of the audience at hand. Put another way, do special preparation for the group you will be with. Is it a school group? A group of writers? A special organization? The particular group addressed should be considered when selecting material to read and questions to ask. This is basic preparation for an event, but many try to do the same presentation for every group—and this simply does not work. Make the extra time to connect with each audience.

At the same time, don't go on too long. Sometimes we get to love the sound of our own voices too much, but there are times when less is definitely more. For those of us who are poets, we can pull out a poem, share it with the group, and get a fairly good, and immediate, read about the reaction of the audience. Pay attention to the response, and this will help guide the length of sessions. After a few events, this will become second nature.

Finally, everyone has a child inside. Tap into that when doing events, especially for younger audiences, and the success will follow. If you don't have fun sharing your work, the audience will definitely notice that. Be yourself—and enjoy the time with your readers!

———

Luis Rodriguez:

Confidence comes with practice. Don't give up. I've made many mistakes in readings and talks. But now with years of experience, I've learned to avoid these, and you will, too. If you do make a mistake or misspeak, just acknowledge and move on. People are really with you. Always keep that in mind.

———

Jeremy Schraffenberger:

It's important to be gracious to your hosts during a reading, so I always make sure to thank them at the beginning of my readings; if possible, I also try to personalize this thank you somehow, saying something specific about the venue or the city I'm in. Planning your own readings can take a lot of time and effort, but I try to remind myself that those people who are inviting me to read also spend a lot of energy (and sometimes money!) preparing things for your event. If possible, I'd suggest that a new writer get involved with a local group, bookstore, library, or organization to help organize a reading. This experience really does give you a greater sense of camaraderie in the literary world. Readings are events where you can sell some books, sure, but they're also meant, I think, to create the kind of connections between people that sustain vibrant literary communities.

Arnold Adoff:

If visiting schools to talk about my books, I like to bring in bags of all my materials, from rough drafts to completed manuscripts, and spread them out on long tables so the kids can see everything that goes into writing a book. I've done this with adult audiences as well, and they also love this. Students, and many adults, don't understand much about the process of publishing, so letting them see all of this really opens their eyes and leads to great discussion. I'll say, "Look, this is my scribbling. There's a napkin from when I was eating in a restaurant and thought of an idea that had to be written down right then." I go through the whole process and share how everything fits together to end up in book form. This is the simplest of "show-and-tell," but it can also get kids involved in events who otherwise might just sit there and do nothing. This also really goes a long way toward bridging the gap between the artist and the readers, to demystify the whole artistic process.

Also, when you go to schools, leave a few copies of your books for the school library so that the kids who can't afford to buy the books will also get a chance to jump into them. This may seem like a small thing, but many of these same kids will later have the means to continue following your work—so this is a great act of promotion of the author's work. It's the small things like this that can bear the largest fruit.

A final thought for new authors: You have to remain on the outside. Writing is always a struggle, and you have to balance between alienating people with power in the publishing world and telling the truth. You must never do mediocre work. If you're an artist, you're an artist. Just do the work in your heart—and share that with your readers.

———

Brad Cook:

Make connections with booksellers. It's the relationships with bookstores that will garner signings and future events. Stop in bookstores in every city you visit and, if possible, introduce yourself to the event coordinator. Leave your business card or something that has your books listed on it. That initial contact can lead to an invitation to the store later on when your next book comes out.

_____

T.C. Boyle:

Well, where possible, give everyone in attendance a crisp new $100 bill. That should do it.

_____

Scott Cawelti:

Enjoy it—it's a great treat for both you and your audience to share your ideas and writing. Feel flattered that people want to hear you and read your work. Most people would love to be writers themselves, and they envy you. Give them your everything at the event. They will appreciate it and remember the experience—and buy your books.

_____

Constance Levy:

Sometimes you can just get carried away with yourself. During a reading to a fourth grade very sharp and focused group, up came the inevitable question, "What inspires you?"(Sometimes it's "Where do you get your ideas?") I proceeded to tell the truth as I always do and may have gotten carried away a bit talking about how I use the poet's eye that we all have if we care to use it. By way of illustration I told about taking a walk down the street and really seeing the richness of ordinary things. I noticed one boy had a puzzled, sort of worried look about him, squinting behind his glasses. "Do you ever...I mean do you..." I got his message. "Ah, I see. You want to know if I ever act like a normal person and just take a walk?" He was relieved to know the answer was yes.

———

Jerome Klinkowitz:

Dealing with discomforting people in the audience can be a challenge. Some years back, at every local reading I'd give for a new book, a malcontent would appear and try to mess it up. He was notorious for being unproductive, having simply appropriated the work of others as his own (and self-promoting it incessantly in the local media). He'd ask annoying tautological questions, trying to make himself the center of attention. The audience would be more bothered with this than I was. Finally, after several events where the audiences were quite upset with this person, I decided to take their side and did a Jack Benny-like shrug and sighing, "Isn't it tragic when cousins marry?" The person never came to another event.

———

Sally Walker:

Reach out to local bookstores, especially independent stores, and let them know you are available and willing to work with them on a book event, visit the store, etc. For example, the "Indies First" program is a good one to be involved with, if possible. Independent booksellers are vital to what we do, and we must do everything in our power to support them.

———

James O'Loughlin:

Give people reasons to buy your book. An inspiring reading helps, but let the audience know what they haven't heard (give teasers) and will have to buy the book to find out. Also, an indication that you are eager to sign and personalize books for people probably also helps with an on-the-fence book buyer.

———

Nikki Giovanni:

Authors worry too much. Just write a good book and, with experience, most things will fall into place.

———

Lee Bennett Hopkins:

Above all, be yourself. Remember the audience you are addressing is there for *you*. As for other advice? Enjoy the experience. You never know who you might help to achieve their life goal. The written/spoken word is so important...your words...words created by you...words never written before.

———

Gary Soto:

Indeed, use this piece as a caution to beginning (and veteran) writers. It's really not sour grapes about not attracting a bookstore audience, but more about my reluctance to get involved in standing before an audience where in the end I sell four or five books. I was once scheduled to do a reading and not a single person showed up—and this included my wife, who wandered off to the magazine rack!

All of us veteran writers have had something similar happen to us, so it would be a great thing for new writers to see that this sort of thing happens to the best of us.

———

QUESTION #8: *What are your funny or unusual "tales from the road"?*

Jimmy Santiago Baca:

Well, here's a good one: Baraka and me are flying at night to upstate New York. We get there in the worst storm ever, an ugly blizzard. On the plane we talked about how the reason we were on the plane, the only two on the plane, was because we had a dozen kids and bills to pay. Anyway, we land, and two ladies pick us up and drive us to the university. The roads are so packed with snow there are no roads, no way to tell where the hell the lanes are—just open, even blankets of snowy hills all around. We get to the auditorium and here's two thousand chairs set out, steel folding chairs, row upon row, and there's these two old ladies in the front holding a warm apple pie on their laps. That's four—our two hosts and these two old ladies. So, we convened at the table on the stage, ate apple pie, and talked poetry—and were then driven back to airport to grab the first plane home. Four people, ha—and two thousand chairs set out. Felt like a Stephen King novel.

———

Luis Rodriguez:

One incident comes to mind: I once read poetry and did talks at the Heidelberg Poetry Festival in Germany. After one such event an Irish gentlemen came up to me, very excited, to tell me he and his wife owned the only Mexican restaurant in Heidelberg. He wanted to treat me to a meal. Of course, I said yes—what were the odds I'd find great tacos in Germany? The place was packed. It looked like Mexican food had a future in Germany—and thanks to an Irish dude. Anyway, he brought me beans and enchiladas. I began to partake, and I must say, it was the worst Mexican food I'd ever eaten. My host eventually came by and wanted to know what I thought. Normally, I'm straightforward and honest. But I just didn't have the heart to tell him what I really thought; he was quite eager to show me his place and for me to approve. I told him the food was fine, thank you, and took a few more bites. It was awkward sitting there, my host across the way with a big smile. I just didn't have the heart.

———

Nancy White Carlstrom:

Back in my earliest days in Alaska I made a number of trips to different communities under the sponsorship of "Authors to Alaska." I remember one time telling the students about my young boys, Jesse and Josh. Later a little girl raised her hand and looking very concerned she asked, "But who is feeding your children?"

Also, once, when doing a large assembly program at a school in Washington state, a student asked if Jesse (main character of many of my books) smoked. Of course not, I said and thought, "Why in the world would he ask that?" Later I wondered if it was because one of my slides showed Alaska natives at a summer fish camp and I had mentioned they were smoking salmon!

Another one of the most memorable comments came from a young girl in Ohio.

After the program she was so anxious to talk with me. She proudly said, "My great, great, great, great, great grandfather bought Alaska!" I can't remember the girl's first name, but of course, I remember her last. Seward!

———

T.C. Boyle:

The long intro is pretty tough. Once I was being introduced by the mayor of a town that will remain unnamed here. I was waiting in the wings. And waiting. And waiting. But he was the mayor and he was beloved and pretty funny. I searched desperately backstage for the hook, but couldn't find it. Finally, I gave up, and when I did get out there onstage I announced that I was going to run against him in the next election.

———

Scott Cawelti:

My newest book, *Brother's Blood,* is about showing how a murderer who insists he's innocent still (after nearly 40 years) is actually guilty and why. A few times during a reading, someone will insist that he really is innocent, and my whole premise is wrong, even though it's based on literally years of research and dozens of interviews. I'm never quite sure how to deal with these people, except tell them to read the book.

———

Constance Levy:

This is definitely not funny and I hope not the usual experience for authors but I am retrieving it from the pit of humiliating moments as an example to others.

I was about to walk up the steps to the podium, notes in hand, to make my award acceptance remarks (for winning a literary award) at a conference very important to me when the gentleman in charge stopped me to say that the featured speaker had just gone way overtime and telling me to "cut it short". Once on stage, I was tempted to tell what had just occurred but my conscience intercepted. If only I had been prepared with a heartfelt and/or witty few words or had at least a bit more time to re-adjust, all would have been well. It was not. It was a mess. Don't let this happen to you.

———

Rob Rains:

One funny story for you. I did a biography several years

ago of Tony La Russa, the Hall of Fame baseball manager. I arranged a book signing during the Cardinals' spring training, outside the team store at Roger Dean Stadium. One lady bought the book and when I politely asked if she would like me to sign it, she said, "Well whose autograph are you going to sign? You're not Tony La Russa." My response was, "Yes, but I am the author of the book." She said, "OK."

———

Jeffrey S. Copeland:

After my book *Shell Games* was published, it received quite a bit of publicity and appeared on several of the "must reads" lists and even in a few bestseller categories. I ended up several times on NPR, on television programs, and did quite a large number of newspaper interviews. At the time, my head got about as big as a Buick. I remember one night my wife called me into the living room to watch television by saying, "Come on in here—if your giant head can get through the doorway." That is, it was that big until I was in line at a local grocery store one day and a woman came running up to me and shouted, "You're him—I seen your picture in the paper. You're that famous guy. Can I have your autograph?" Instantly, a small crowd started gathering, and I thought to myself, "This is pretty cool." The lady produced a small sheet of paper from her purse, handed it to me, and said, "Gary, please sign it to Rosie—that's me." Well, my ego shrunk to the size of a pea when it came to me she thought I was Gary Kelly, the incredibly gifted artist who illustrates children's books and does many of the paintings and illustrations for Barnes & Noble (he was also all over the news at the time). So, what did I do? I signed the piece of paper for her:

"To Rosie, with love.....Gary."

———

The advice and suggestions shared above are offered as "food for thought" for authors while individual presentation styles are created and honed. Again, a final piece of advice is for authors to experiment with the suggestions that seem most appropriate or practical to them as they begin (or continue to refine) preparing for book events. These experiments, no matter the result, will in so many ways help provide the foundation for the successes all authors hope to achieve.

SECTION 5

And Now a Word from Our Sponsors: Advice and Wisdom from Bookstore Event Coordinators

> "Where is human nature so weak as in the bookstore?"
>
> —Henry Ward Beecher

While authors speak about their books in a wide variety of venues and for many audiences (libraries, with book clubs, schools, organizations, and so forth), there is absolutely no doubt the individuals who spend the most time with them while they are sharing information about their books are the bookstore event coordinators. From the initial planning stages all the way though the events themselves, perhaps no other group has the range of insight into what authors do to help create entertaining, informative, and successful (and, sadly, at times the not-so-successful) experiences for those who gather to hear about their latest work. The event coordinators, from this unique perspective and through their experiences, are, therefore, the true experts in the area of creating successful book events and are in the best position to offer valuable advice and suggestions for new(er) authors.

What follows now are the "voices of experience" and "best practices" advice from event coordinators representing bookstores among the finest in the country. They also represent a full range of the different types of booksellers and venues where book events take place. Each of these individuals was asked to respond to any or all of six questions posed to them about their experiences working with authors before and during book events. In the case of a few of the questions, the responses of the event coordinators were quite similar (especially in regard to the need for authors to build in an audience by bringing family and friends to book events).

Rather than eliminating this duplication, these similar responses are being kept here, as-is and by design—to provide emphasis to one of the most important aspects of building successful book readings and events. These comments are also being kept to show authors that event coordinators generally consider this near the very top of the list of "musts" to be attended to before events take place. Thus, in the comments below this may at times seem like a broken record, but it is also a song that event coordinators believe authors cannot hear often enough.

Finally, the advice and suggestions are presented here in a "Roundtable Advice" format for each question, a structure that should make the information easier for authors to access when building their own book events.

Event Coordinator Roundtable Advice

QUESTION #1: *What are the most important ways to build success for book events?*

Corey Mesler, Burke's Bookstore:

After scheduling author events for over 30 years now I still feel like saying, "I have no idea what works and what doesn't." One of the first signings I ever hosted was for the romance author, Rosemary Rogers. At that time, pre-Grisham, she was the number one selling author in the world. We had six people show up for her signing, which left me a lot of time to flirt with her.

The best events, naturally, are with local authors. Our three best signings in the last year were for Robert Gordon's book on Stax Records (a Memphis institution and international sensation), Alan Lightman (who was born and raised in Memphis) for his book *The Accidental Universe*, and Heather Dobbins (a Memphian) for her first book of poetry. And all of these fine folks did their own groundwork, emailing friends, contacting media, and generally knowing what they were doing during the event, which included handling advance orders for signed copies, and helping us shape the evening in an appropriate way, balancing signing time with reading time. And, it helped us feel good about what we are doing because each of these three showed public gratitude for the event. That is appreciated.

———

Christopher Blaker, The Book Lady Bookstore:

I have very specific thoughts in this area. The authors who are self-motivated and aid in doing their own press/publicity tend to do well. Next, if your book applies to a particular group or demographic, for example the military, reach out a local post/base and make sure they are aware of your book. Know your potential audience and try to reach them. This can be a key to a successful event—or one poorly attended.

Also, plan as far ahead as possible. Don't call a bookstore a week before you want to do an event and then get frustrated because the store couldn't get something together on short notice or the event was poorly attended. Never forget that print publications need advance notice for event announcements. Finally, bookstore employees tend to be busy and juggling multiple things, so if you don't get a response directly, follow up a second time to see if the store is interested in hosting an event.

———

Kris Kleindienst, Left Bank Books, St. Louis:

Authors who have successful events contact their local friends and family in ample time with an event invitation and encourage their friends and family to support the event buy purchasing their book *at the hosting store*.

Authors should also provide the bookstore well *before* the event with a good quality author photo, jpg of cover art, bio, reviews—and a couple of comp copies.

The most successful authors don't have a party

first with all those above named at someone's house or restaurant and give everyone the book. This pretty much undermines any hope of local sales.

The most successful also tweet, post on Facebook, and provide information about the event on their website. They also link to the bookstore's e-commerce website on their website so that people can purchase the book online. They DO NOT steer people to an Amazon page while expecting the bookstore to be basically a free reception venue.

Finally, they listen to and respect the requirements and requests of the hosting bookstore as to what makes a good event.

———

Candy Purdom, Anderson's Bookshop:

The authors who conduct successful events share a taste of their books, but do not tell *everything*. The best ones give information about how the book came to mind, and how they approached writing it. Also, give some teasers to spark interest, not unlike what movies do with trailers or TV shows do to entice viewers to tune in. If a reading is to be done from the book, it can't be too long. Maybe two short passages is the limit. And they are willing to engage with the fans and take questions for a period too. The author/program can take 30-40 minutes, with questions. It should be wrapped up in an hour and then the booksigning line begins. They SHOULD NOT tell everything about the book. Examples: we had one author, a prominent newsman, come for an event. His book was about the death penalty and contained cases and outcomes. It was a rather short collection of cases, and I recall that he told about every single one. I had purchased the book myself ahead of time and then wondered why I did! I no longer needed to read it. And on the other side: one of our authors was a Munchkin in *The Wizard of Oz*. He had actually been a carnival barker as a kid (the guys who would shout out about the freaks, and atrocities, or the scantily-clad women that ticket buyers would see if they paid the price for a sideshow ticket). He knew *exactly* how to sell his book. Everyone here wanted to get details about Judy Garland, but this kindly little old gentleman would only talk about *his* life, and with regard to Judy Garland he'd say, "Buy my book, and you'll find out about Judy Garland." He got it!

Another thing we're seeing more of now is that authors bring PowerPoint presentations. They show images and talk about their books. That works too, as long as they still engage with the fans, make eye contact, and address them in the program too.

Also, during the signing period, we always help with personalizations by using Post-It notes. So if the reader wants a "To Mary" or a "To Tim," our staff writes that out and puts it on the title page to help the author with spelling. Let the staff know ahead of time what page you prefer signing and if you are willing to personalize and/or pose for photos. Some do, some don't, but there's no changing it midstream!

Another good idea is to bring swag, if you can

afford it. Some publishers are wonderful about sending bookmarks, or rubber bracelets, or mini posters, or tee shirts, or something. Or they bring a gift of some kind to raffle off to the attendees.

Many authors also do their own social media campaign to their online fans. That's a big boost too, and we appreciate that very much AS LONG AS they have a way for fans to buy their books from the hosting bookseller. It's very discouraging to have people arrive here with a book they've already purchased and they then expect to get signed with us. Not cool! The only way this whole author book tour thing works is when the author sells books, and the publisher is happy, and the bookstore that is running and staffing the program sells enough books to make it worthwhile. We want happy authors, happy customers, happy publishers, and happy bookstores. Group hug!!!

———

Jeremy Garber, Powell's Books:

The #1 thing authors can do prior to an event or reading is to focus their energies on securing an audience. While bookstores often do their own promotion of upcoming events, social media is an invaluable tool for authors to reach both established fans and new ones. Authors that do social media promotion and outreach in support of their events often enjoy greater turnouts than initially expected. While traditional media remains important (review coverage, event listings, etc.), the role of social media cannot be understated.

———

Dana Meister, Full Circle Bookstore:

It's really quite simple. The authors have to be obnoxious (I mean that in the best sense of the word) about promoting their book to fans, family, friends, and even strangers. They have to take advantage of every opportunity to sell not only their book, but also themselves. To me, that is the only difference between successful and not-so-successful signings.

———

Maryelizabeth Hart, Mysterious Galaxy Bookstore:

First, not all authors read well. Author, know thyself.

Shorter readings are better 95 percent of the time. Authors should practice the introductory material to the piece they are selecting to read, not improvise, which often includes rambling and hesitation to avoid spoilers.

———

Ginny Wehril-Hemmeter, Anderson's Bookshop:

Authors with the best events spread the word! They really tap into their audiences directly and let them know where they will be signing, especially if they are local to a certain store. It's great that you are connected to your fans, but that doesn't always translate into sales if you don't talk about your events.

———

Jay Schwandt, Carmichael's Bookstore:

Successful authors tell all their friends and family to come to the event. Our number one success story with events (unless there's national name recognition like a David Sedaris) is author participation with regard to marketing. A bookstore alone cannot get folks to come to an event, especially for an unknown author. When an author aggressively promotes the event with his/her contacts and tells all their family and friends to attend, we have the best results. Assume we (the bookstore) will get no one to attend your event. Of course we do what we can, but if you start with that assumption, we have much better success and everyone walks away happy. Never assume that hundreds of people will magically come to your event only because an event is scheduled.

———

Suzy Takas, The Book Cellar:

From my experience, authors who have the best success at readings talk about their book and writing process but do not spend a ton of time reading the actual book. The conversation should intrigue us to read the book. A peppy, vibrant speaker always helps.

If you are an instructor, be sure to have your students attend the event. This helps fill the room and create a much better atmosphere there because the students already know you and will eagerly participate in discussion.

———

Annie Leonard, The Next Chapter Bookstore:

They keep the presentation short (15 minutes or so). They also keep it engaging with personal/insider anecdotes, and they reach out to the audience and get them involved as much as possible in the event and discussions. Also, activate your network of friends, neighbors, acquaintances, etc., and help the bookstore market your event.

––––

Robin Theiss, STL Books:

My strongest suggestion would be to choose a passage to read that will hook the audience and read it dramatically. At the same time, charm the socks off the audience by engaging them before the reading with a brief intro, one that includes some humor or personal anecdotes and includes a little about how the book came to be. That always seems to work well.

––––

Debbie Cross, Antigone Books:

The authors who have the best events are generally local authors who have their book launch with us—which means their true launch (and haven't previously even done a wine and cheese party thrown by a generous friend). A city the size of Tucson can generally have one successful event for a local author, but when there are two or more, sometimes that just spreads out the crowd and creates several smaller events. A local author who actively promotes her or his event (emails, Facebook, etc.) is hugely important. We help out as much as possible, but they have the contact information for their circle of friends and associates, which is key.

_____

Richard Howorth, Square Books:

The most successful authors are well prepared for their presentation, know whether their work is better suited for reading or simply talking about, and know how to connect with the audience rather than perform for them. They also have a good sense of timing—whether a certain passage is too long, which questions need a short answer and which might require a longer answer, know how to deal with people in the audience who are "talkers" when they are supposedly asking a question, and know when to stop.

_____

Amanda Sutton, Bookworks:

I have two suggestions. First, authors should do as many interviews as possible with the local media (and in surrounding areas as well). Second, post fliers everywhere possible and put notices on social media.

_____

Sam Barry, Book Passage Bookstore:

Authors who promote their event well ahead of time in every way they can, and do not simply rely on the efforts of the bookstore, have the most successful events. Authors should, where possible, contact the local newspapers and other media outlets to see what type of publicity they might be able to do. Newspapers will typically do at least an announcement for the event if given enough advance notice. Bookstores will often do this, but the author should also see what could be done with the media.

———

Owen Hill, Moe's Books:

Come prepared! If the event includes a reading, choose two short excerpts that will interest even a casual reader. Read the first, then gauge audience interest. If you "have" them, read the second excerpt. Otherwise, a good Plan B is to go to Q&A or talk a little about the writing of the book. Engage the audience! Ask them a question, say something nice about the venue...personalize.

———

Pam Grange, Kepler's Books:

My number one piece of advice: Don't give away the ending (fiction) or your conclusions (nonfiction). I've seen this done way too many times. Authors must, first and foremost, entice listeners to buy the book.

———

Cindy Norris, Malaprop's Bookstore:

The most successful decide in advance if a "reading" from the book is the right presentation. Second, authors should practice in front of real people who will be honest with them about the speaking abilities—like relatives and friends. Take suggestions to heart, and work to improve. Finally, practice with friends asking them questions. Q&A is often the most interesting part of the evening, and the author should be very comfortable with it—and this comes with practice and experience.

———

Ronnie Carrier, Green Apple Books:

I'm sure you've heard this from others, but authors who promote heavily through their social media outlets (Facebook, personal webpage, twitter) have great success. Also, local authors tend to draw larger crowds, so we very much enjoy hosting them.

Many who have great success also do more than just read from their book. For example, they have PowerPoint presentations to show. Or, and this can be great fun, they have other writers come to the event to read the author's work being touted.

———

Stephanie Schindhelm, Boulder Book Store:

Do NOT rely solely on your publisher or on the bookstore to promote your event. If you have fans in an area, you need to let them know that you are coming, so put it on your website, put it on social media, do everything you can to let any local contacts you have in an area know that you are having an event. While a bookstore will alert their customers to your event, you must not forget that your target audience may not be people who are typically in a bookstore or on a bookstore's newsletter list. The most successful events we have typically happen when both the bookstore and the author are doing everything they can *together* to promote the event.

———

Dorothy Pittman, Horton's Books:

Authors should provide a detailed contact list to the bookseller as well as personally contacting family and friends about the event. From my experience, the most successful authors who do readings at our store have prepared in advance and find a common ground with the audience they can build on at the event. They look at the local news and find out what is going on in the area and incorporate that into the talk.

———

QUESTION #2: *What have authors done while the events were taking place that helped make them more interesting, informative, and enjoyable?*

Stephanie Schindhelm, Boulder Book Store:

The best presentations I have seen authors do typically include a mixture of talk about the book (the writing or research process, interesting stories about writing it, perhaps a bit about the publishing process), and short readings from the book. I would recommend reading a little from the book, so people can hear your words in your voice, but I would discourage most authors from reading for longer than five minutes. The only author I've seen who could do this was Neil Gaiman. Many people have a very hard time listening to someone read aloud for very long, so if you want to read more, intersperse the readings with other things. Thirty minutes is an ideal length of time for a presentation (this doesn't include Q&A). We have found for our events that the best timeframe for a presentation is a 30-minute presentation and 15 minute Q&A, followed by a signing. It's shocking how dramatically sales of the author's book will drop if the event lasts longer than 45 minutes.

———

Christina Bittner, Read Street Books:

Many suggest inviting family members and relatives to events to help swell the ranks of the audience. This is a good idea, but remember that relatives too often do not purchase the book. Therefore, to get others to the event, authors need to market, market, market themselves and their books. I would suggest that they build a giant Rolodex of contacts with local radio, television, and newspaper contacts will help them get the word out. I wrote local columns for the *Baltimore Sun* and the *Maryland Gazette* and was always looking for topics; a local published author was an ideal topic, so I always looked forward to hearing from them. In the end, I would say build an audience—and go after people who will purchase the book. Unfortunately, those who publish need to be writers *and* salespersons.

At the same time, here's another suggestion. If the author's work is nonfiction, I strongly urge teaming up with a teacher or professor from a local college who can speak on the subject matter in the book. Having another "expert" along in the areas being talked about can really change the atmosphere of an event, in a wonderful way. Plus, the other "expert" can also answer questions from the group—*and* ask the author pre-arranged questions—which will enliven the discussion.

———

Candy Purdom, Anderson's Bookshop:

The authors address their fans, engage with them, are patient with questions, and the stories fans tell them. Those authors who share enough, but not too much. They repeat a question loud enough for everyone to hear. They don't rush out of the store as soon as they possibly can! It's the WORST when that happens, and it *has* happened. Authors decide they need to leave, and strand fans who are waiting for them. That makes EVERYONE unhappy. We had one author who insisted she had to leave at 9 p.m., leaving maybe 30 people standing there waiting. Why did she leave? She had been out the night before until some ungodly hour and just was worn out. Now, it seemed to us, who had planned this event with her for weeks, that she might have taken her confirmed calendar into account while socializing the night before. That was very unprofessional.

———

Kris Kleindienst, Left Bank Books, St. Louis:

First of all, thank the store for having you there, and remind folks to support the store and its staff. Also, plan ahead what to read and say and practice speaking slowly and audibly so that the audience doesn't have to work hard. Don't be shy but also don't be a shameless droning-on-and-on self-promoter. Be someone folks like.

If possible, consider springing for some refreshments, especially if this is your hometown crowd.

———

Annie Leonard, The Next Chapter Bookstore:

The most successful at doing events engage with readers, especially through a good Q&A session. Be sure to listen carefully to what is being asked, and then try to give a response that will be easy to understand. Usually, one question leads to another, so don't give up on these sessions if hands are slow to pop up. Most people are very shy in settings like this, so you'll have to wait them out. However, once a question has been asked, the floodgates can open and a great session will follow.

———

Steve Olsson, Barnes & Noble Booksellers, Waterloo, Iowa:

It seems the authors who are best at talking about their books have a sales mentality. They are practiced and confident speaking to small and medium-sized groups, and seem to have a "stump speech," a planned (and possibly even practiced) sales pitch for their book and themselves.

———

Suzy Takas, The Book Cellar:

Sometimes a prop helps. Bring a picture or an object related to the book that can be shared with the audience and talked about. Or, if an author has one, consider sharing an interesting related life story—one related to the book. Also, if possible, book trailers or other types of video related to the book are great to show while waiting for the event to begin. These trailers build a great climate for a talk.

———

Ginny Wehrli-Hemmeter, Anderson's Bookshop:

Come prepared. If you are going to read, choose a passage ahead of time and practice reading it until you are completely comfortable with it. Also, be ready to answer questions and be gracious to your guests, even if there are only a few people present—which *will* happen at times. Ask your publisher to make you some swag bookmarks or other goodies, which are hot commodities and are an extra incentive for someone to come out and meet you.

———

Richard Howorth, Square Books:

It can't be said enough that authors must have a good sense of the audience, and know how to connect by being spontaneous, humorous, engaging. Usually the more relaxed the author is the better things go. Make as much eye contact as possible instead of being glued to your remarks or text. Much of this will come with time and practice. Just be yourself, and enjoy the experience.

———

Sam Barry, Book Passage Bookstore:

Choose a compelling passage from your book to read aloud. It need not be the beginning of the book. Don't make it too long—10 to 15 minutes is about right. Introduce your reading, speaking extemporaneously, providing a context for what people are hearing. Listening to a passage being read aloud is different than reading it—your audience can't re-read what you are reading to them; some of them may need a bit of help understanding what they are hearing. Practice your reading ahead of time. Then open it up for questions. People like to ask questions, and often want to hear about your writing process. Be prepared to share that.

———

Rene Martin, Quail Ridge Books:

Don't talk or read too long! Give the audience enough of the story to whet their curiosity but not so much that they have no reason to buy the book. The author's main job is to build up interest, and nothing kills that interest more than a long, drawn-out event, especially one loaded with "spoilers" for the story.

———

Peter Maravelis, City Lights Books:

Intention is everything. Arrive at the venue in a motivated state. Prepare. Authors need to engage the audience. They need to learn stagecraft. If this is daunting, they shouldn't be speaking in front of groups—but focus primarily on methods of promoting their book online.

———

Robin Theiss, STL Books:

First of all, smile a lot. Make eye contact with people in the audience—many do not. Finally, try to make a personal connection with each attendee, even if that means asking *them* a question about the topic of the book.

———

Amanda Sutton, Bookworks:

Consider the comfort level of the audience. Are the chairs arranged so everyone can hear and see? Is the room too hot or too cold? Are chairs spread too far apart to achieve good discussion? Authors and event coordinators should work together to make sure the location is as good as it can be for the event.

———

Dorothy Pittman, Horton's Books:

Talk with the customers, especially *before* the event starts. Then, during the presentation, speak slowly and loudly enough for everyone to hear what is being said. Take the time to answer as many questions as possible. Finally, keep the discussion on target. Too many wander from the reason the event is taking place!

———

QUESTION #3: *How should authors prepare for events?*

Gretchen Treu, A Room of One's Own Bookstore:

Show up early and be patient and friendly with the staff! Many would simply not believe how poorly some authors treat those who work at the bookstores. The bookstore staff is there to help as much as possible, and a kind word is greatly appreciated.

Next, mobilize your networks! It's really author outreach to their professional and personal networks that makes events successful for us (in terms of both attendance and book sales).

Plan ahead! Contact potential bookstores at least two or three months before your book is released. Seriously, that is always best, but most authors don't think about that. In addition, be prepared to handle book sales on a consignment basis if you are from a tiny publisher or are self-published.

Authors should also have PR materials, including a professional-looking high-quality author photo, book jacket, as well as all of your preferred social media contacts and reviews of your book, in one place so that you can provide those items upon request. Finally, link to the bookstore on your own website/social media. (Amazon isn't the one hosting your reading, after all!)

Kelly von Plonski, Subterranean Books:

They reach out to their fans, friends, family, and co-workers using every means at their disposal: word-of-mouth, social media, phone calls, e-invites, email. If it is a relatively unknown author, strangers are generally not going to come to an event. It is always the author's fan base who show up and the author has the most direct line to those folks. The bookstore can send out press releases (subject—always—to the whims of the journalist), email their mailing list, and use their social media, but those are just shots in the dark. The author needs to tap her finger on the head of her fan/friend/co-worker/family member and say, "Hey, I expect you to show up."

———

Stephanie Schindhelm, Boulder Book Store:

The number one most important thing for new authors to know is that you are the best advocate for your book. In this day and age, when there is less and less money for marketing from the publishers, it is very likely that if you want anyone to discover your book, you are going to have to do a lot of legwork on the marketing side. This is the thing that I hear from authors again and again at events. They thought the hard part would be writing and getting the book published, but for many, the real hard work begins after publication because they weren't prepared for all the marketing they would have to do.

The second thing isn't advice so much as just something important for authors to know: events aren't free for bookstores to host. Most bookstores don't have dedicated event spaces, so when they host an event, oftentimes they have to close down a portion of the sales floor for two or even three hours, depending on how long it takes to get the space ready. Then there is the time of the booksellers to run the event, set up the space, create displays (which are usually in windows or in main traffic areas, which means these are very valuable spaces for a store), create marketing materials, do promotions, not to mention the cost of any outside marketing a store might do like a newspaper or radio ad. All in all, events can be very expensive (for our store, the average event costs us about $500). For this reason, many stores are now requiring a co-op fee from the publisher to help alleviate this cost (our store asks for $200) and this will likely be the case more and more often in the future.

———

Lisette Howe, Read Street Books:

This may sound like a small thing at first, but many authors simply do not read aloud well—and a poor reading can ruin an otherwise excellent event. For those who don't read aloud well, I recommend bringing along, if possible, a friend who *does* read aloud well to read the passages that will be shared with the audience. People actually love this, and it takes away a concern shared by many authors. These "designated readers" can be family members, other authors, friends—or even members of the bookstore staff if they are given enough advance notice so they can practice reading the passages.

———

Christopher Blaker, The Book Lady Bookstore:

Just because an author writes a book doesn't mean people will magically know about it. The author (this applies especially to self-published authors) needs to tell people about their book, in every way possible, and where to get the book. We have a number of self-published books on our shelves that we've never sold any copies of because the author thought, "Well, I've written the book, I can take it easy and watch the money roll in." It just doesn't work like that.

———

Ginny Wehrli-Hemmeter, Anderson's Bookshop:

Advice for new authors: PLEASE direct your fans to purchase your book at the venue at which you are speaking! I can't tell you how many times people come to our events with a book purchased elsewhere. The author/publisher/bookseller cannot afford to have author events if there are no sales to prove it makes anyone any money. This includes links on your website to places other than the Big A, and information to your fans about the array of places to pre-order once a book is announced. I'd also ask an author to make sure that they are doing some publicity on their own; you can't rely on the venue to do everything, and covering all your bases never hurts.

———

Kris Kleindienst, Left Bank Books, St. Louis:

Make sure you have an easy way for bookstores to order and carry your book. Many authors don't realize it, but most of the time it needs to be available at full trade discount with returnable terms from Ingram or Baker & Taylor at minimum. Bookstores cannot carry a billion one-book accounts with tiny or self-publishing companies. It is simply way too expensive.

———

Peter Maravelis, City Lights Books:

Authors need to learn more about vaudeville. As Groucho Marx once said: "Say the magic word, and the duck will come down." Once you enchant your audience, they will reciprocate. Don't just stand there and "lecture" an audience. Involve them in every way you can—and have *fun* with the event. So many authors appear too rigid and formal, and they look like they aren't having any fun at all. If that is the case, this can turn off a group quickly. Think in advance of events what could be done to enliven the presentation, and be creative with this.

———

Steve Olsson, Barnes & Noble Booksellers, Waterloo:

The most important piece of advice I would give to authors is that after they have set up a reading or event, the job isn't over until that night; the work has just begun. Don't assume that the bookstore/library will have the time and/or resources to promote your event aggressively. Don't assume that people will flock to your event just because you have written a book. You need to network as much as you can. Contact newspapers and radio stations. Local papers are often reluctant to pursue running a story about an upcoming book signing when they receive it from a bookstore because it seems less like a story and more like an attempt to get free advertising (which, in point of fact, it is!). They most generally are more receptive if the story idea comes from the author him/herself, so the author needs to take care of this. This is just one of the truths of the business, and bookstores need the help of the authors in this area. Finally, invite all of your friends, family, coworkers, etc. It may feel like a cheat to you, but having lots of people around (even though YOU know that they all know you) creates interest in other people.

————

Deborah Horn, Barnes & Noble Booksellers, Fenton, Missouri:

Authors need to understand that simply showing up will not sell books. Customers these days are immune to authors, especially in bookstores that host a lot of signings. Unless you are Stephen King or Stephen Hawking or Stephen Colbert, buyers are not going to be impressed by a sign in the entry or the sight of you sitting expectantly at a table. They must already know about you or your book. They must have come to the store BECAUSE of your book; otherwise they will simply walk past you. Most likely they will give you a wide berth to avoid being "sold to". This is why it is so important that you create your own buyer list by promoting your signing in advance and developing an email list.

Understand that bookstores have guidelines they must work within. Those guidelines may be very different from store to store (even with a chain of stores), but they will have solid reasons behind them. Remember that the store's goal is the same as yours—sell as many books as possible. That's why they are picky about what signings to host and how to host them.

––––––

Candy Purdom, Anderson's Bookshop:

Arrive a little early to meet the staff, get to know them, and let them know if you need any special help getting set up for the event. Be ready with your program. Also, appreciate your fans—even if they are few! Some events just won't have large crowds, for a variety of reasons.

Also, before leaving, ask the staff if there are any other requests *they have of you*. At times, the bookstore will also want you to sign books which did not sell at the event so that they can be put on the shelves as "author signed." Thank those at the bookstore for their help. Some authors write personal thank-yous, or even send goodies. The most remarkable act I recall by an author—and he was also a big celebrity—was that he called us the next night to thank us again. A random staff person answered and they were delighted to hear from Henry Winkler just calling to thank us for such a wonderful night!

––––––

Robin Theiss, STL Books:

Ask not what your host can do for you, but ask instead, what you can do for to promote yourself and the event.

Recognize you're not there to sell books, but to sell yourself. If you sell yourself, the book sales will follow.

Finally, don't worry about the size of the crowd. Focus instead on building a connection with each attendee. There is a lot of power in one devoted fan. Authors should never forget that.

———

Jay Schwandt, Carmichael's Bookstore:

Don't read the entire book during your event. Read *only enough* to entice folks to buy your book. Then take questions. Sometimes short and sweet is the way to go. Some authors read and read and read and read. That's too much. It kills book sales.

———

Suzy Takas, The Book Cellar:

EVERYONE has had an event with a small turn out. However, it is still an important event. Those people who did attend will tell their friends about what they did and saw and heard and the ripple about the book begins. Even if the event is small on the actual day, that event has been on a website for a month, it has been sent in an email, it has been tweeted and posted on FB. The book is out in the universe and the only reason things have occurred is because an event was scheduled.

———

Annie Leonard, The Next Chapter Bookstore:

My biggest piece of advice, especially if the author is self-published, is *before* coming to do an event, work out the details with the bookstore as to pricing. If this isn't done in advance, much confusion and wasted time can happen the day of the author's appearance. Also, ask the bookstore if it is possible to leave signed copies, consigned copies. Sometimes that will be possible and beneficial to all.

Finally, as many others have said, know that many readings/events don't get a good turnout. Treat all of those who do come as if they are important.

———

Debbie Cross, Antigone Books:

Authors should know the bookstore they are approaching to host their event. Do some research beforehand and find out the types and range of books the store sells—and the types of events they typically do. Also, authors should support the store by placing links to the store on all author websites used. This will be greatly appreciated.

Authors should be prepared to supply the books for a signing if they are not easily obtained by other means.

Prior to their event, authors should try to get their book reviewed, be on a radio or local TV show—and if so, DEFINITELY mention the date, time and location of the event.

———

Richard Howorth, Square Books:

If there is an opportunity to meet people in the audience BEFORE speaking or reading, take advantage of that. In your own way, be friendly and outgoing to people, try to shake hands, etc. The more the audience feels they know you before you talk, the more interested they will be in what you have to say. Before reading or giving the prepared talk, try to open spontaneously, make remarks about where you are, talk informally about what you've been doing, just as you would if you were making the acquaintance of people who had just walked into your kitchen at home.

———

Rene Martin, Quail Ridge Books:

A classic mistake for new authors is trying to have a reading at every single venue they can possibly think of. This results in many small events rather than one or two large successful ones. Therefore, authors should map out a *strategy* for how many events to conduct in a given area. This is so important.

———

Corey Mesler, Burke's Bookstore:

We have hosted signings for local writers who just expected their friends would show and almost no one did. If from out of town, ask the bookstore what you can do to help with promotion. Some authors feel very comfortable talking to the appropriate media representatives, and some will even contact those representatives if given emails or phone numbers. Also, don't expect a crowd at every stop and, if one stop doesn't seem as good as others, don't tell the bookstore that. It sounds like common sense, but there are a handful of writers I would rather not have return who spent a good part of their visit carping about the low turnout. Finally, show your love for the bookstore no matter the size of the crowd, and thank those at the bookstore for their effort to help with the event; many authors forget to do this.

―――

Emily Stavrou Schaefer, Schuler Books & Music:

This may seem odd advice—and it is not meant as an advertisement—it's meant merely as a look at other possibilities out there for self-published authors. If those who were first planning to do an e-only book are interested in print copies as well, we, and many other booksellers across the country, offer publishing services. For instance, and just as an example, we offer publishing services through our Espresso Book Machine with low minimums, one offs, etc. Not only do I think that this is a great opportunity to bring in INDEPENDENT bookstores into this project, but also helps with a lot of writers who are new to the process and aren't very tech savvy. The bookstore staff involved with this can be a great resource for authors interested in having print copies.

Also, in terms of other advice, go to readings at bookstores prior to your own. I can't emphasize this enough. Most self-published authors who reach out to me for events have never even been to an author talk.

Learn about the format, and take notes. A compelling presentation sells books!

_____

Cindy Norris, Malaprop's Bookstore:

Relax, smile, know your work, and be able to talk about in from many angles. Be able to talk in detail about how you wrote the book or conducted your research for it. People like anecdotes about the "adventures" authors have on the way to getting a book published, especially those involving obstacles that had to be overcome before the book became a reality. A good story-behind-the-story will go a long way toward getting the attention of an audience.

_____

Ronnie Carrier, Green Apple Books:

PROMOTE PROMOTE PROMOTE PROMOTE—and then promote some more!

Also, if it is within the rules of the bookstore, remember this: the older crowds like wine and beer. A lot. The bookstore won't be able to provide these, but the author, in some cases and situations, can. Be sure to ask the bookstore representatives about the "rules" for bringing in food and drink. And, crowds of all ages like snacks and pizza, which are much easier for an author to supply if the rules permit.

In addition, make flyers and posters for the book and event—and have them put up all over the area where the event will take place, especially in libraries, coffee houses, and other places readers typically gather. This may seem like a great deal of work, but this can also make the difference between a small crowd and a standing-room-only group.

———

Anna Bongiovanni, Boneshaker Books:

It is important, when possible, to pair up with another author whose book or work is similar in theme or style with yours. This works really well if you are a visiting author and don't know many people in the city. Pairing with a local author on an event will automatically bring a small crowd of people who know their work and other locals. If you don't know an author in the local area, ask the bookstore if they can think of someone who might be a good "partner" for you at the event.

It's important to make sure flyers about the event look interesting and are designed well and go up around town (especially around the building where the event is going to be taken place). Bookstores will appreciate it if authors can send some of these *in advance of* the event to be posted in the area.

———

Mary Williams, Skylight Books:

The thing that bookstores really count on authors to do is to get the word out to their own mailing list of contacts in the area. While bookstores do a lot of promotion to their own audience, they rely on authors to help and reach out to their friends, family, colleagues, and readers.

———

Dorothy Pittman, Horton's Books:

The author should *not* give away copies of the book in the local area if he/she wishes to sell copies. Many do this and then wonder why sales are slow at the bookstores the day of events!

———

QUESTION #4: *What are reasons behind not-so-successful events?*

Christopher Blaker, The Book Lady Bookstore:

Check the dates to make sure your book event does not conflict with another, perhaps a more popular event— i.e. a music festival. Authors should research this before working with the store to schedule an event. Also, do one event per area. Don't cannibalize your events by having two in the same area around the same time.

———

Richard Howorth, Square Books:

Pitfalls: Author reads a passage that is too long or reads too many passages. Author reads in a "dramatic" voice, or tries to dramatize characters' voices, when the author is not good at doing that. Author rambles when answering a question. Often the audience is shy about asking questions—give them time, pause, say, "Well, this is an uncomfortable silence," or anything to break the ice. Q&A is usually the best part of an event. Keep your reading or remarks short enough to allow time for questions.

Anything over 30 minutes total for reading and Q&A is too long unless you're really nailing it. When people start getting up and walking out (though some have a legitimate reason to leave early) it's usually a sign that you've gone too long.

———

Gretchen Treu, A Room of One's Own Bookstore:

Don't be rude to the bookstore staff, including the event coordinator, if something goes awry. Things sometimes just happen. Be gracious and thank the store for hosting your reading. Be friendly and courteous to your audience members and make sure you make yourself available to questions and to having your book signed. Many times authors' family and friends descend upon them after the reading, which is natural, but do your best to make sure that strangers get a chance to connect with you. After all, they have come to purchase your book, too!

———

Candy Purdom, Anderson's Bookshop:

Plan to arrive in the place you're expected! Sometimes New York publicists don't have a clue about distances. Find out where you're going and get there on time! Weather and traffic issues have messed us up many times, and it's maddening! Also, it's important to con-firm all of your program details before heading out there. If the author expects a projector and screen and laptop, etc. for a power point presentation, they'd bet-ter make sure it's available. Some stores may have those things, some don't. If they need a particular kind of pen for signing, or if they need a special kind of sparkling water or only brown M&Ms, they must let the stores know. (But being picky about backstage needs is a hassle, to be honest.) Just know what's expected of you and tell the bookstore what you expect is my best advice.

_____

Kris Kleindienst, Left Bank Books, St. Louis:

Some potential pitfalls: Author did not publicize. Author held a previous private event. Author held too many events in one community and diluted the possible audience.

The author's book may be of interest to the author's immediate friends but is not of the quality to gain credibility in the mainstream market and simply does not attract new readers to an event. (This is actually the biggest misstep: thinking that because you wrote it and paid someone to print it, that it is of equal value and quality to what is published professionally. BE REALISTIC.)

_____

Stephanie Schindhelm, Boulder Book Store:

There are a number of factors that can play into a not-so-successful event, some of which you don't have a lot of control over (the weather being #1 on that list). But the two main factors behind not-so-successful events are lack of an audience, and not letting your audience know about the event. The first is something that I do what I can do to avoid. If I don't think there's an audience for an event in our area, I typically won't schedule it. The most annoying reason though is definitely when the event is for a local author, and the author doesn't let their local contacts know about the event because they feel self-conscious about promoting themselves. If you have gone to the trouble to set up an event at your local bookstore, and they've gone to the trouble to create displays, order in your book, and do other promotions for your event, you need to tell everyone you know to come support you (and tell them to bring their friends and family!). The pitfall new authors fall into is assuming that since they have a book published, everyone knows they have a book out, and assuming that all they need to do to have a successful event is to set up an event.

———

Rene Martin, Quail Ridge Books:

This isn't exactly a pitfall, but this is something we do— and authors should check into this before contacting bookstores to see if they would be willing to host an event. Checking on this will save everyone a great deal of time. We do *not* offer events for books published through Createspace or any Amazon publishing arm. It is a business decision not to support the company that is trying to put us out of business. This is not saying we won't support a self-published book, just not one published by Amazon.

———

Dorothy Pittman, Horton's Books:

A big pitfall: the author, prior to the event, gave away free copies so there is no incentive for family and friends to attend the event. Also, do not misrepresent local connection—any author living 100+ miles away from the event location is not really local. Finally, know your audience and remember that just because you wrote a book does not mean it will sell. Authors must really *work*, using all means possible, to build an audience.

———

Margot Sage-El, Watchung Booksellers:

First of all, when approaching independent booksellers, do not direct them to obtain your book from Amazon. That would be a terrible thing to do. Your website should list indiebound.org or your local bookseller as a source for purchasing the book.

———

Steve Olsson, Barnes & Noble Booksellers, Waterloo:

Sometimes, people write a book and then just expect that people will be automatically clamoring for it. They do no work ahead of time and then blame the venue when they are embarrassed with a poor turnout. The venue is on your side; they want a big turnout, too. Oftentimes, the store/library has no budget, no time, and very few channels to pursue to promote your event. At those times, it's on your shoulders and you will need to carry the load.

———

Deborah Horn, Barnes & Noble Booksellers, Fenton, Missouri:

Pitfalls to avoid: Many new or generally unknown authors just sit behind a table expecting customers to rush up to them begging to buy their book. We all wish it were that simple.

Also, this isn't thought of that much by authors, but it most certainly should be—poorly designed, unattractive covers on books. Just like food: the presentation is half the appeal.

Finally, unprofessional behavior by the author or the author's entourage. A book signing in a store is *not* an excuse for a family reunion.

———

Jay Schwandt, Carmichael's Bookstore:

Frankly, I'm not a fan of self-publishing. Often the quality of the physical book is lacking, sometimes the cost of the book is way too high (in comparison to other similar books published by major houses). One mustn't judge a book by its cover alone, but many people do. And will. Though this won't affect an event, particularly if the author aggressively promotes it, it may impede continued sales and contribute to a languishing shelf life. Bookstores are drowning in requests by local authors who have self-published. It's a bad, bad way to go, in my opinion. And some of these self-publishing companies really gouge the author.

———

Annie Leonard, The Next Chapter Bookstore:

Poor timing, poor advertising, poor fit of the author's work to the community. In terms of potential pitfalls, authors shouldn't talk about themselves too long during the event—unless the personal information is directly related somehow to the subject or content of the book.

———

Maryelizabeth Hart, Mysterious Galaxy Bookstore:

Talking about one's Amazon sales is incredibly poor etiquette and makes readers, and bookstore representatives, visibly uncomfortable. *Definitely* avoid this.

———

Owen Hill, Moe's Books:

Don't go on too long. Be aware of the audience. Are they sleeping? Has anyone left the room? If you are doing a signing, don't linger in conversation with one person. If any old friends show up, make arrangements to meet them later. You have (hopefully) a line of interested customers. Close the deal!

———

Anna Bongiovanni, Boneshaker Books:

Don't, as some authors do, expect the bookstore to do the work for you. Often they have limited time/energy/money and can only promote so much. Often I've heard people talk about an event that just happened at the store and someone will exclaim, "I would have totally gone to that if I had known about it." Also, make the event interesting and creative. Think about pairing up not with just another author, but maybe an expert in the field that you are writing about. Or a poet or an artist. Lastly, don't have your event go on too long. An hour is a good amount of time, with an hour and a half tops. Anything over that is pushing it.

––––––

Robin Theiss, STL Books:

Major pitfalls I've seen through the years: Author made no effort to promote the event in advance. Author showed up alone and relied solely on the event host to provide the audience. Author did not seem prepared, did not have a good intro to the reading. Author failed to thank the host (plug the store, etc.). Author did not engage the audience with humor, personal info, etc. before and after the reading.

The material read was poorly selected, did not hook the audience. The reading was too short or too long. Authors should ask bookstores for help with these areas, especially if authors are new to doing events.

––––––

Suzy Takas, The Book Cellar:

Biggest pitfalls: Not bringing their own people to the event. Not posting about the event. Sometimes events fail because of bad weather, beautiful weather, playoff games, parades, and other community happenings that you just cannot control. A dry, uninteresting reading.

––––––

QUESTION #5: *In which areas should authors and bookstore personnel work together before events to help make them successful?*

Michael Keefe, Annie Bloom's Books:

When considering whether or not to book an author for a reading here, what I like is an email that is concise, but also tells me most everything I need to know in the first email. Many authors provide only summaries of their book, and possibly author bios. While this is important, we care just as much (and maybe more) about authors' marketing plans and their potential to draw a good crowd. So, tell me whether or not you're a local author. If not, do you have friends, family, and/or lots of fans in the area. Are you reaching out to local media? Another very important consideration for us is book availability. Out-of-town authors on small presses are, unfortunately, very tough to accommodate, simply due to distribution. For local authors, we often consign books (see: http://www.annieblooms.com/book-consignment-info). For out-of-staters, however, the terms from a small publisher are often prohibitive. And even getting distribution through Ingram often doesn't work for us, because they don't provide a great discount to begin with, and they charge restocking fees on returned books. So, it's helpful for authors to let us know how we might be able to get their books and to offer as many alternatives as possible for getting them.

———

Candy Purdom, Anderson's Bookshop:

Be clear about your program. Remember your audience and that the store is likely open for business during the presentation. So if you are going to be throwing out F-bombs as you discuss your book, remember we have members of the public around. Any promotion to friends, family, college pals, targeted groups of readers can only help! The store does its best to reach folks who would be interested in your book, but if you have the means to do that type of thing, be our guest! I do sometimes think authors (especially first-time local authors) see that we get hundreds of people to our book events. And they assume, if I just take my book to Anderson's, those people will come because that's what they do at Anderson's. Nope, sorry. The associative property of author events is not a real thing. A might equal B, but it does not always equal C!

———

Margot Sage-El, Watchung Booksellers:

Booksellers review thousands and thousands of book descriptions each year from publishers and carefully make selections and order the books they think will interest their customers. When sending out inquiring emails about whether the store would like to host a book event, please provide a brief synopsis (one paragraph is sufficient) about your book. That way the bookseller can determine if the title fits their demographic or not— and whether an event would be appropriate—and can respond to you.

Also, don't forget, inquiries about the possibility of doing a book event should include your outreach. Who is your target audience? Is there a local group/organization that would support such a book? Include your marketing approach, and ask the bookstore what they do.

———

Robin Theiss, STL Books:

Authors should send publicity materials to the event host. This includes author headshot .jpg image, book cover jpg image, author's bio, high res book poster/flyer, and list of interview questions with author's answers. This can make a quick and easy blog article).

In addition, authors should plug the bookstore or venue where the event will take place in all pre-event publicity. Also, as a gesture of thanks—continue plugging them after the event.

Authors should also provide the event host with a list of things the author will be doing to promote the event with an offer to do more (e.g., bring someone along to assist with the signing, bring some bookmarks, candy, food, etc. for attendees).

———

Michelle Fleegel, E. Shavers, Bookseller:

The best thing that an author can do before a reading or event is to get some publicity in the local newspaper. Sending the appropriate person at the newspaper a copy of the book is a major start with this. Newspapers will most often work more closely with the author for the publicity for an event, so authors need to take the initiative in this area.

———

Amanda Sutton, Bookworks:

Authors should help make sure ordering is easy and at the benefit of the bookstore, whether books are brought in direct from the publisher or with the author. Please consider that event coordinators get dozens if not hundreds of emails and phone calls per day. Keep your communications concise and minimal. Confirm the date and work with them on ordering and check in about a month out, but don't over-communicate ahead of time.

———

Christopher Blaker, The Book Lady Bookstore:

Give the store plenty of notice and send a copy of your book so they can look over it. It helps if a store employee reads and likes your book; then the employee can use word-of-mouth to encourage people to come to the event. Never underestimate the influence of the bookstore staff. If they like the author's work, they can really help with the promotion of an event, especially with regular store customers.

———

Dorothy Pittman, Horton's Books:

Prepare and send the bookstore a short bio and press release. At the same time, write a short and very brief summary of the book so that the bookseller will be able to hand-sell it. If the bookstore has "rules and regs" for authors, study them carefully and do not try to get around or ignore them.

———

Maryelizabeth Hart, Mysterious Galaxy Bookstore:

One of the most common questions authors are asked, after questions about workdays and process, is who they like to read. Authors who are prepared for this question often can contact the host store in advance to be sure the store has inventory of whomever they're recommending. This, too, helps the bookstore sell books, and all will be most appreciative of the extra effort.

———

Jay Schwandt, Carmichael's Bookstore:

You shouldn't schedule twenty events in town. Schedule one event, call it a "book launch," serve wine, cheese, goodies, and invite everyone you know. One well-promoted event does more good than dozens of readings with little to no promotion. This will also make the event worthwhile for the bookstore and everyone involved.

———

Suzy Takas, The Book Cellar:

If at all possible, have other authors or an author that has an established audience in the area tweet about the book and/or event. It is easier to rave about someone else than it is to rave about yourself. Authors should work together and help each other out when planning events. That only makes sense.

———

Annie Leonard, The Next Chapter Bookstore:

The best thing an author can do to help the bookstore is to market the event! One of the best ways to do this is a special mailing to your friends and relatives, either electronically or by regular mail (some do both). We've worked with several authors who had special invitation cards printed up that they sent to specific people, to add a personal touch to the invitation process. Taking this extra time really helped them build audiences for their events, so the extra effort was worth it.

———

Richard Howorth, Square Books:

Do some research and find out what the store's pre-ferred format and time for events is—and try to picture what the environment will be like. Ask them whether they prefer reading or just talking and Q&A. Bookstores are always happy to visit with authors about such things. Also, find out whether the event will be in performance atmosphere, or will you be someplace where you're competing with people walking around, telephone calls, and sounds of cash register, etc. Find out if there's a sound system and let them know whether you prefer one (sometimes you need it, other times not).

———

Emily Stavrou Schaefer, Schuler Books & Music:

All authors should create an electronic press kit. Provide a press release, hi resolution author headshot, bio, book cover image, and synopsis of the book. Those authors who also provide self-written introductions are a step ahead of the rest!

———

Pam Grange, Kepler's Books:

We do a lot of promotion at our store, but the best way to get a crowd is for the author to promote to everyone they know—and definitely use social media; e.g., Facebook, Twitter, email lists, etc., etc.

———

QUESTION #6: *What are the most unusual happenings you've seen or have been a part of while hosting events?*

Robin Theiss, STL Books:

We once had an author come in early to pre-sign books at Barnes & Noble in Ladue prior to an event where we expected a large turnout. The store set up a table and chair with stacks of books. In his haste, the author somehow overlooked that one of the stacks wasn't his books! They had evidently been set on the table by store personnel in error. The store ended up with about 20 copies of another author's books, signed by someone else!

———

Christopher Blaker, The Book Lady Bookstore:

No one said writing was easy or fun. Even if you work hard and do everything right, there can be unsuccessful events. This event did not happen at our store, but the author verified that it did happen.

The author had published his first book. He had an event scheduled in January at a Connecticut Barnes & Noble. He drove two and a half hours through a snowstorm from where he lived in New York City to Connecticut. When he got to the store, it was only empty chairs. Eventually, a woman who was all bundled up from the cold came in and sat down. So the author started his reading for this one woman. At the end the woman thanked him, explained that her heating unit had gone out and she came to the bookstore to get warm and that if the book ever came out in paperback, she might buy a copy. After saying that, she left.

The author, Georges Dawes Green, has three successful novels under his belt now, two of which were made into movies. My point: don't get discouraged.

———

Kris Kleindienst, Left Bank Books, St. Louis:

The funniest event I can remember was with a mainstream author. Partway into her event, the fire alarm went off because of a small kitchen fire in the adjacent restaurant. It was very, very loud and only the fire department could turn it off. We decamped to the sidewalk, complete with a rolling cart with books and a cash box and waited. The author, a comedian, did a pretty good job of keeping us all entertained. When the fire trucks arrived, the event turned into a photo op with the firemen and author. Moral: when life gives you smoke, light up!

———

Richard Howorth, Square Books:

Lot's of crazy stuff has happened over the years. Not sure this is the funniest, just the most recent. At a poetry reading a couple of days ago a customer sort of stumbled into the event. We're in the South; she was obviously a Southerner. She was dressed in the colors and symbols of the local university's athletic teams (including earrings, socks, an apron, a bunch of those Lance Armstrong bracelets but in the school colors. She walked up to the rear of the event and said, quite audibly, "What is this?" Someone told her it was a poetry reading. After the first poem she held her arms up, waving them and rapidly snapping her fingers. People looked at her and she said, "Don't you know? This is the new way of *clapping!*" After the second poem was read, she said, "Well, I've got two words to say about that: DAY - YAMN!" When the poet began explaining that the following poem was related to the poet's insomnia, she immediately volunteered, "Don't tell *me* about insomnia!" After the next poem the poet began to explain that he is a Northerner, and she interrupted by loudly chanting the school's fight song—and telling the audience "the words are *right here*, on my apron." When the manager finally began to explain this was, after all, the poet's show she said, "Well, just call me a peckler." A peckler? we asked. "Yeah, that's like a heckler but for a poet." We decided the peckler was, on balance, a good thing.

―――――

Dorothy Pittman, Horton's Books:

It is not really funny, but we did have an author drive through the pouring rain to have a signing at our annual "MayFest" event. When half the vendors did not show up and it looked like the lightning and rain would continue, the event was cancelled. Unfortunately, he was already on his way, and we were unable to contact him. He showed up, and so did a couple of his favorite fans who braved the rain to see him. One of the food vendors was still selling BBQ, so he was able to get some BBQ for his fans and take some home with him.

―――――

Maryelizabeth Hart, Mysterious Galaxy Bookstore:

MG has been hosting authors for events for more than 20 years, in all sorts of circumstances, including deluges of rain (yes, in Southern CA!), fires, and accidentally against a significant sport playoff game on occasion. One event that still stands out in memory, from our very early years, is the late William Murray spontaneously breaking into song—in full operatic voice—to the delight of the attendees. What a day that was!

―――――

Steve Olsson, Barnes & Noble Booksellers, Waterloo:

We had a signing at our store for a regional author who had ties in our town, but was not from here. He had written a very good nonfiction book about a very traumatic event that happened here 50-60 years ago. In speaking about his book, he lamented that he had not been able to speak to a certain person who owned some wreckage related to the event, and that that person had been "stonewalling" researchers for decades, etc. When he finished speaking and went to questions, it turned out the stonewaller's son was in the audience—and the son launched into an impassioned defense of his father and his reasons for keeping the object to himself. Thankfully, the author had actually been fairly restrained when speaking of the father, or it could have been even more uncomfortable. I guess the moral is, never assume that its safe to speak ill of someone when doing an event in their hometown!

———

Deborah Horn, Barnes & Noble Booksellers, Fenton, Missouri:

I wouldn't exactly call it "funny," but it is a sort of morality tale. I once hosted a signing for a *New York Times* bestselling author who happens to live locally. This author lives on a large, secluded piece of property in the county just south of our metro-area. The people of that county have a reputation for being unsophisticated. She grew up in that unsophisticated area and married two different men from there. In what I can only guess was an attempt to distance herself from the perceived country bumpkin life, she made several very derogatory comments about the county and the people living there. It was bad enough that she would say these things in public at all, but what was worse was she was wearing a microphone and customers throughout the store could hear her. She was making fun of the entire population of a county that represents half of our customer base.

Needless to say, she will never be invited back to this, her hometown bookstore, to sign books.

———

Candy Purdom, Anderson's Bookshop:

We had a children's author in for a signing, and bookstore staff were doing post-it notes at the signing table to help with personalizations of books. I had a dad who explained his daughter's unusual name. When I asked what his daughter's name was for personalization, I heard, "Zennifer, just like Jennifer but with a Z." Okay, weird, but doable I thought. That can be figured out. NO, I heard him say, Z-e-n-n-y-p-h-y-r. What? In my head I now thought, "That's nothing like Jennifer with a Z. Jennifer with a Z, I could do. And who could do that to their child? A lifetime of spelling her wacky name, that her parents think is clever. Poor kid." There is also a lesson here for all authors and bookstore reps: Always ask for the correct spelling of a name before a book is signed!

———

Ginny Wehrli-Hemmeter, Anderson's Bookshop:

One funny event was when we were hosting a music celebrity who is originally from our area. One of his ex-girlfriends showed up to the event! It was awkward for a moment, but he laughed it off.

―――

Suzy Takas, The Book Cellar:

One female author wore a mustache to appear like the main character in her book. Robin Sloan told a great story. Simon Tofield drew pictures on a big easel.

A group of poets read each other's poetry instead of their own. All were very clever—and quite entertaining.

―――

Stephanie Schindhelm, Boulder Book Store:

One of my favorite local authors is Gail Storey, whose book, *I Promise Not to Suffer*, is about hiking the Pacific Crest Trail with her husband, having never done any serious hiking before. She is not only an engaging and funny storyteller, but she's also an amazing promoter of her book and our store. At her event, she had a costume of her book that she wore, along with hiking boots and a tiara, and she packed the house and sold ALL of the books we ordered (as well as 20 more copies she brought from home). During the holidays, we had her come in to the store as part of Indies First on Small Business Saturday (the Saturday after Thanksgiving), and she not only helped customers find books (while wearing the cutest Santa dress), she also sold a ton of her book. We had her come in every Saturday after that for the rest of the holiday season to sell her book at the front of the store, and we sold over 100 copies during the holidays.

———

As in the previous section devoted to responses from authors, the advice and suggestions shared above are offered as "food for thought" for authors while individual presentation styles are created and honed. A final piece of advice here would be for authors to experiment with the suggestions that seem most appropriate or practical to them as they begin (or continue to refine) preparing for book events. These experiments, no matter the result, will in so many ways help provide the foundation for the successes all authors hope to achieve.

SECTION 6

Photo Gallery

The photos and captions in this section are provided to help illustrate points made throughout the book—points provided by bookstore event coordinators, authors, and from my own experiences. The photos also represent just how enjoyable and rewarding book events can be for everyone involved if the time is taken to prepare for and build successful events.

Essential partnership for building book events: bookstore event coordinator and author. Shown here, one of the best and most creative event coordinators: Deb Horn, Barnes and Noble, Fenton, Missouri.

The signing table. Note books, bookmarks, author business cards, and cake!

Another signing table, this one with examples of objects related to the book spread out upon it so that those in line can examine them while they wait.

"Signage" promoting the event is important. Always work with the event coordinator to make sure signs and fliers have the specifics of the event.

When doing book events in venues other than bookstores, try to bring along signage that will promote the bookstore that helped organize the event or came to sell books. Note the banner in background here that let everyone know a local bookstore helped with the event.

Ask bookstores if they will make a special exhibit for the new book a week or two before a book event is to take place. Customers will take note of the exhibit, and many may decide to come to the event because of this type of promotion.

"And how do you spell your name?" Always ask for the correct spelling of the name before starting to sign the book. Always.

Keep the line moving. At times, the line of those waiting for an author's signature will grow quite long. Decide upon special inscriptions to include with the signature before the event. This will help keep a steady pace during the signing.

Visual aids related to the subject/content of the book can greatly enhance the interaction with the audience. Here, specific types of shells are shown—related to the subject matter of the book Shell Games.

A cake with the title of the book or an image of the book cover on it is always a crowd pleaser. Enjoying food while information about the book is shared creates a relaxed, and fun, atmosphere at events.

Many will want pictures taken with the author. Ask some of these individuals to send you copies of the pictures so you can add them to author blog and websites.

"Location" for the event in the store (or other venue) greatly influences how easily, or how difficult, it is for those in the audience to hear you, even if a sound system is used. Try to stay as far away from doors as possible so that distracting sounds don't interfere with the presentation.

When doing book events in other countries, give strong consideration to bringing along your own equipment. For this event in Birmingham, England, I brought my own laptop, power adaptors, and related cords (with special connections for outlets).

Bookstores are busy places, so members of the staff will generally not be able to sit with you at the signing table for long periods of time. Therefore, keep the table arranged and organized so that you can be self-sufficient while greeting your readers and signing books for them.

National conferences (the National Council of Teachers of English conference in this photo) are great places for authors to promote their books.

Always be thinking "outside the box" for book events. For those who write nonfiction, consider working with museums, history groups, and other appropriate organizations to take readers to locations important in the book. In this photo, readers are being taken by bus to specific locations described in Shell Games, *and a short reading followed at each stop.*

Readers can also be taken on walking tours of sites important to the story; this type of event is quite popular and can be quite memorable and great fun for all involved.

At every turn possible, try to involve the media in promotion of your work and upcoming events. The publicity gained can help make the difference between a small group and a standing-room-only crowd.

Network with other authors and entertainers, both to help promote your books and events and to acquire photos for author blogs and websites. Here, I'm on stage (in the middle) with the "Po' Lonesome Boys" bluegrass band, one of the best in the business.

Make time for yourself. One of the perks of the travel for book events is getting to explore new places. Here is the classic photo of "holding up" the Leaning Tower of Piza. Enjoy all the experiences that come with book events!

Book signing events held outdoors are always subject to the quirks of the weather. Always take large umbrellas or a portable canopy just in case they are needed. Here, signing as part of a town festival.

Always the unexpected... Difficult to see from the picture, but due to a much larger crowd than anticipated showing up for a signing, I was placed at the last minute in the only space available in an historic museum: on a platform on an elevator shaft! My signatures were a tad shaky that afternoon.

Promotion through the media is always an important part of letting others know about new books. However, authors must take the good with the not-so-good in this area. This particular newspaper ran a feature story on my new book, but on the front page they decided to shorten the title (Ain't No Harm to Kill the Devil: The Life and Legend of John Fairfield, Abolitionist for Hire) *and put it next to a picture of me. Thus, it is quite clear right on the front page who the Devil is! Actually, many found this to be quite funny, so it did help with sales of the book.*

A FINAL WORD OF ENCOURAGEMENT

> *"Success is liking yourself, liking what you do,*
> *and liking how you do it."*
> —Maya Angelou

It has long been said about me, "He never met a microphone he didn't like!" That is true. I genuinely love being in front of an audience and sharing information about my books because books truly do help make the world a bigger and better place—for both the audience and the author. And when people gather to talk about what is inside the pages of a book, information is shared and discussions take place that often open new viewpoints, deepen understanding, make people question old beliefs, and, at times, start the process of great change in how lives are lived. The connection, the bond, between author and audience offers the potential for joy, for tears, for laughter—and many times a thorough combination of each.

Learning to create this atmosphere with a group takes effort and practice, and for some writers this can take some time to achieve. As much as I love being with groups of readers now, my own readings were not without bumps and potholes in the road. I once spent an entire month preparing for a book event tied to a cele-bration being held by a town. The subject matter of my book matched perfectly the theme of the local celebra-tion. However, a serious outbreak of the flu in that town caused those in charge of the event to cancel every-thing—only they forgot to inform me! After a two-hour drive, I showed up to an empty auditorium. The event was never rescheduled. At least I didn't catch the flu!

At another event early in my career, right after my introductory comments, a local author raised a hand, asked a question, and then kept talking the rest of the time set aside for the event! At that time, I didn't know how to handle such a situation, and my presentation never got off the ground.

At still another event, the bookstore that was to bring copies of my books completely forgot to do so, and I had nothing to offer those who wished to make purchases, some of whom had traveled over a hundred miles to hear me speak! And, like many who provided advice for this book, I have also had events where just one or two people showed up— leaving me to have very nice, personal visits with those who did make the time to attend.

Were these events failures? Not in the least. These sorts of things just happen, and authors must take them in stride and use them as opportunities for learning and growth.

Far overshadowing the potholes, there are moments both during and after events that authors will always hold dear—moments that help demonstrate just how meaningful an author's work can be to those in an audience. After I conducted one event, a young woman came up to me, tears in her eyes, and hugged me tightly. When she finally backed away, she let me know she was the niece of one of the individuals I had written about, and my book had filled in a hole in her family history the family had always wondered about. She further related that through the years her family had drifted away from each other, but the book had brought them all back together again with a stronger bond than ever.

Another time, a couple of weeks after my reading at a high school, a teacher forwarded me a letter written by one of her students who had enjoyed my presentation. The student's comments made me very happy, but it was what the teacher wrote that I remember to this day: "To my knowledge, yours was the first book he has ever completed, and now all he wants to do is read!"

About a year and a half after another reading, a reading held during a horrible snowstorm, I received a package from a young man who had braved the weather to come hear me talk about a new book. In his letter, he said that listening to me that night was the spark that finally got him started writing his own book, which had just been published and a copy was inside the package. I opened the book, and my name was right there in the Acknowledgments. I'll never forget that moment - ever.

Most events fall somewhere between the potholes and the smiles, but the potential is always there to make a great impact on the lives of those present. This potential should never be wasted. Authors should—no, must—put forth the best effort possible at each and every book event. We can't know if there are those who might be out there in the audience who will be so touched and moved by our words that their lives could be forever changed. Preparing for these events is hard work and doesn't come easy to everyone. However, you can do it. Have confidence, take action, and you will do it.

While time and experience are great teachers, new authors don't start out with the benefit of either. I hope this book will be a help to you. Before you "hit the road," make the time to study the sections of this book and experiment with the different recommendations that seem most appropriate for both your own personal style of presentation and the particular type of book you have written.

With a good foundation for knowing how to create and work with others to create the events, you will be able to have the experiences you dream of. Also, the appendices that follow have been designed to help you attend to the essentials that build toward success before, during, and after events. Take your time to prepare, and then invest your best effort, knowing full well that time and practice with each event will make it all much easier and more effective down the road. Finally, don't worry if your first book events don't go exactly as you had planned. Those first events seldom do. Do your preparation, then just get out there and do the best you can. It will become much easier with a little time and practice. It will!

Your book is a gift to the world, and each event is your opportunity to showcase that gift. Even for the most prolific of authors, there are long stretches of research and writing between the releases of books. Therefore, enjoy and savor every single minute of this time you are able to share with your readers. And, as you do, I wish you all good fortune, wonderful experiences, and many books in your future.

APPENDICES

Appendix A: Query Letter Template (for notes to bookstores and other groups)

(Note: Please feel free to use this template as-is —or adapt to your own purposes)

Template:

Date

Dear (name of event coordinator),

I am the author of (title of your work), which has recently been published by (name of your publisher/ publishing venue). (Title of your work) is (describe your work here—no more than five or six sentences, and make it as interesting as possible!).

I am writing today to ask if you would please consider having me to (name of bookstore or other venue) for a book event and signing. I believe an event at (name of store or other venue) would be beneficial for both of us. I'm currently in the process of promoting (title of your work) and would appreciate another opportunity to do so. At the same time, I feel I can provide an interesting and enjoyable experience for your (customers/members/or other group(s) to be addressed).

I am particularly interested in doing a reading/book signing or a special presentation (mention the other types of presentations, if any, you are also willing and able to do there). However, I'd also appreciate it if I could discuss with you which type of event you feel would be most useful and beneficial for (name of store or other venue) at this time.

I understand the importance of building audiences for events, so I would also be happy for us to work together to help create a broad range of publicity for the event.

I thank you for your consideration and look forward to visiting with you about the possibility of a book event at (name of store or other venue).

Sincerely,

Your name
Your mailing address
Your e-mail address
Your phone number(s)

Your author blog, website address, and/or other sites if appropriate

Final note: If a response is not forthcoming in a few weeks after the note is sent, place a follow-up call to the individual to whom this was addressed. Use the fact that the note was sent as an icebreaker and as a way to get into a conversation about the possibility of doing an event there.

Appendix B: Equipment and Materials to Take to Book Events: A Checklist

The equipment and materials an author will need for an event can vary depending upon a variety of factors, including the type of audience that is anticipated, the particular venue where the event will take place, and even the type of presentation the author chooses to do. However, while preparing for an event, it would be wise to examine the following checklist when assembling the equipment and materials. All on the list may not be needed, but checking through the list *before* an event may prevent an author from discovering *at* an event that badly needed items were left at home or at the office.

Checklist: Which of the Following Will be Needed for the Upcoming Event?

_____ Ink pens for writing autographs and inscription inside the books

_____ Business cards

_____ Bookmarks

_____ Bottled water

_____ A copy of your book with marked passages to be read to audiences

_____ Note cards and/or printed copy of the presentation

_____ A quality digital camera

_____ Laser pointer

_____ Electronic equipment essentials if book presentations will involve visual or audio components.

    _____ Laptop (and power cord)

    _____ Projector

    _____ Extension cords

    _____ Electrical power/current adaptors

    _____ Back-up flash drive and CD containing your presentation

_____ If bringing any type of food/treats to the event, the following should also be brought along:

    _____ Paper plates

    _____ Napkins

    _____ Utensils (plastic forks and spoons)

Appendix C: Bookmark Samples

Below are sample bookmarks modeled after the "template" described in Section 1. Please feel free to use the format and design of these bookmarks as models for preparing your own bookmarks.

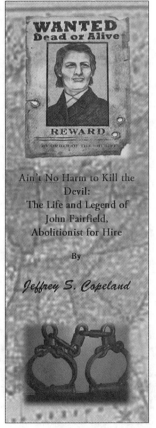

This is the bookmark for Ain't No Harm to Kill the Devil: The Life and Legend of John Fairfield, Abolitionist for Hire. *Both the front and the back of the bookmark are shown here.*

This is the bookmark for Shell Games: The Life and Times of Pearl McGill, Industrial Spy and Pioneer Labor Activist. *Both the front and the back of the bookmark are shown here.*

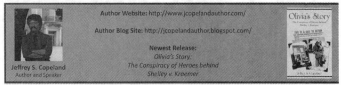

This is the front of the bookmark for Olivia's Story: The Conspiracy of Heroes Behind 'Shelley v. Kraemer—*as an example of how different the front can be designed.*

Appendix D: Building an Audience: A Checklist

Note: *This checklist is specifically concerned with building an audience for events at bookstores. However, the same actions and principles apply if the event is to take place for special interest groups or organizations.*

Of everything done by an author before a book event is to take place, nothing today is more important than helping to create an audience for that event. What follows is a checklist of activities to perform and groups to contact well in advance of a scheduled event. Not all of these will be appropriate in every case. However, the list below is a good place to begin when authors and bookstores work together to help make sure events achieve excellent attendance.

Checklist:

_____ Have fliers and posters been created for the event? And, do these have all the pertinent information about the time, location, and other specifics related to the event?

_____ Has a "targeted mailing" been done (either by the bookstore, author, or both) to special interest groups in and area/region who might be interested in the subject matter and content of the book?

_____Have telephone calls been made to, or e-mails sent to, officers of local/regional groups and organizations that might be interested in the subject matter and to extend a personal invitation to the event?

_____Have television and radio stations in the area/region been contacted about helping promote the event?

_____Have all local/regional newspapers (both traditional and online) been contacted about helping promote the event?

_____Has the author and the bookstore publicized the event by using all means of digital/electronic communication? This would include, but is not be limited to, the following: Facebook, Snapchat, Instagram, Tumblr, Reddit, Twitter, Twitch, Vine, LinkedIn, and Pinterest.

_____Have author blog sites and author websites been used to provide information about and promote the upcoming event? Has the bookstore's included details of the event on its website?

_____Has a *YouTube* video (or other type of video) that would provide information about the book been considered for promotional purposes?

_____Have other bookstores and booksellers in the area (including university and special interest bookstores) been contacted about helping with the publicity for the event?

_____Have the local and regional libraries been contacted about the event? Have these been asked to post fliers and posters about the event?

_____Have book clubs and reading groups in the area/region been contacted about the event? Have special invitations been delivered to them?

_____Have writers groups in the area been contacted and invited to the event?

_____Have the appropriate individuals in the schools (at specific levels), both public and private, been contacted about and invited to the event? Have these been asked to post fliers and posters for the event?

_____Have the author's friends, relatives, co-workers, and acquaintances been invited to the event (to help build in numbers and friendly faces!)?

Appendix E: The Presentation "Opening"

The template below is to be used with "Building Rapport with the Audience" in Section 3.

These comments are given *before* the main presentation begins. Feel free to use the template listed below as-is (and simply fill in the blanks with your own specific information)—or use it as a place to begin creating your own "opening" by adding to, or subtracting from, the template. Remember: Comments such as these should be given to show your thanks and appreciation, so these are a very important part of your talk.

Template: The Presentation "Opening"

Good morning (afternoon, evening) everyone! I have a few things I'd like to say before we start visiting about (title of your book).

First, I'd like to thank (name of event coordinator or other person in charge of the event *and* the store name or other group involved) for inviting me to be here with all of you today. I really appreciate this opportunity, and I also realize it took a great amount of work to get the event organized. Therefore, if you would please, join me in thanking (name of person(s) in charge). Let's give her/him a round of applause.

I'd also like to thank all of you for coming to hear about my book. There are many demands upon our time these days, so I'm grateful we can spend this time together.

I'm also especially grateful to be here because (fill in the blank with how wonderful the bookstore or other venue is, the town and/local area). This is a great place, isn't it?

OPTIONAL: Finally, I want to mention (add a *short* anecdote or story about your connection to the store, group, or area. Humor is always good, but heartfelt reflection will also do just fine).

Again, I thank all of you. Let's now turn our attention to (title of your book).

NOTE: At this point, begin the presentation you've prepared for this particular event.

Appendix F: Sections of the Author Website—A Checklist

There seem to be just about as many different styles of author websites are there are authors—*as it should be*. An author's website should be done very professionally, but it should also make a statement about who the individual author is and the types of writing she/he does. In short, the website should be tailored to be interesting, informative, educational—and fun to browse through. Some sites are incredibly elaborate and detailed; others are quite simple and to the point. Regardless of which type an author decides to use, there are a few elements of the sites that are most common, and these are listed below.

_____ **Section 1: The Home Page**

When you create your website, or have it created for you, remember above all that it must be easy to navigate. Therefore, there are important pieces to include right on the home page. First, there should be a "welcome" from the author that says a few words about what people will find as they browse through the pages. This should be a friendly, inviting welcome to the site.

Next, there should be a good quality, high-resolution image of the author somewhere on the page. A recent publicity photo would be fine, but any representative picture will do. Some authors even like to put a humorous photo of some type to fuel the interest of the readers.

The home page should also have a high-resolution photo of the cover of the author's most recent book—and either a blurb about the book or a review.

Finally, and most important of all, there should be some type of a "navigation-bar" or "menu" that will help direct individuals to the different parts of the site. Again, easy navigation of the site is a must, and this will help with that.

_____ **Section 2: About Me**
The "About Me" section can be either short or long, depending upon how much the author is willing to share about her/his personal and professional life. Many authors give a mini-biography of sorts, starting with early childhood and working up to the present. Others show their lives and careers in pictures, which can be great fun (a writer friend of mine even included her high school prom pictures!). Still others, those who do not wish to provide as much personal information, will talk about their beginnings as writers and show, again through pictures, how they got to where they are today.

_____ **Section 3: Photo Gallery**
The Photo Gallery section is exactly what it sounds like. Here, authors present *both* their lives and works in pictures. There may be some overlap with the "About Me" section, which is fine, but the Photo Gallery most typically shows the author at book readings and events—and shows off the different places the author has been.

Readers love to see into the lives of writers, so this is a very important section.

_____ Section 4: My Books

This section has photos of the front covers of the author's books (and other publications if appropriate). Representative summaries and reviews should also be there as well so that readers can see what each individual piece is like. Most think of the My Books section as an advertising page, a place where an author can tout just how wonderful her/his books are and why they should be read. Also, in the end, this section serves as a "visual bibliography" of the author's work.

_____ Section 5: Invite Me to Speak

This is an OPTIONAL section because some authors prefer to have this area taken care of by her/his publisher or agent. This section typically tells the types of presentations the author is willing to do about the books and which audiences/groups she/he will meet with to do these. For example, an author might list a preference for meeting with schools or various types of civic organizations. Still others might enjoy working with writer groups and/or reading groups and book clubs. Again, this is an optional section, but if the author would like to add this extra promotion, it is appropriate and usually effective in helping the author acquire speaking engagements.

_____ **Section 6: Links**

The Links section should provide hyperlinks or other means for readers to get to an author's blog site or other "Internet-based" materials. Links to YouTube videos about the author's works are very common. Others link to various media accounts and descriptions of the works (interviews, both audio and visual, in particular). The most important consideration here is to keep the links functional and working properly, so regular maintenance will be required.

_____ **Section 7: Contact Me**

In this section, the author should provide the preferred means to be used when readers would like to make contact. The traditional means is to have readers write to the author in care of the publisher. It is perfectly fine to have this as the primary means of communication. However, as the technology continues to change and evolve, many writers are not inviting readers to contact them through the various social media platforms. Still others provide a link to an e-mail account devoted specifically for this type of communication. The rule of thumb here is simple enough: Establish with the readers the preferred means of communication, and then check those areas often, especially as "time-sensitive" invitations to speak to groups often show up in the messages.

———

Please feel free to use the checklist above when constructing the author website. Again, there are many different models, and authors should study what others have done. Then, after careful study, draw up a few plans and run them by readers and other authors for examination. Finally, build the website—and know that changes will always be needed as additional publications are added to an author's bookshelf. Author websites should be seen as "always changing," so don't fret too much about the initial version. Get a site up and running, and then just make changes as needed.

Appendix G: Promotional Postcards Used to Help Generate Audiences and Announce New Books

As mentioned in Section 1, a "traditional mailing" can also be quite useful in announcing an event and helping to generate an audience. One of the most inexpensive and successful means of doing this is by sending specially designed postcards announcing an upcoming event to targeted individuals and specific organizations that might be interested in the event. Most of these postcards have a nice visual representation of the book—often the book cover—on the front as well as specific information about the time and place of the event. The back is generally reserved for a brief personal note of invitation.

While these postcards are quite useful in getting the word out about an event, they are also, with a slight modification, helpful in another important area as well. By simply removing the specific information about the event, these same postcards can be sent to bookstores and special groups across the country to announce the release of an author's new book. Again, the back can be used for a short personal note. Bookstores are constantly bombarded with information about new books, so a personal note of this type can make quite an impression —to the author's advantage.

Note: Please make sure to check with local postal officials about the requirements for "size" of the postcards so that extra funds are not required for mailing.

A sample of both types of postcards is listed below. The first one is an example of the type mailed out to targeted individuals and groups to announce book events. The second one was mailed out to help promote the book *Finding Fairfield: The Behind-the-Scenes Story of Ain't No Harm to Kill the Devil: The Life and Legend of John Fairfield, Abolitionist for Hire*. Please feel free to use both as models for creating your own promotional postcards.

....

The secrets roll along with the Mississippi.....

Shell Games

The Life and Times of Pearl McGill, Industrial Spy and Pioneer Labor Activist

Jeffrey S. Copeland

Pearl's story as a young woman in Muscatine in 1910 through 1912... a story and program that you won't want to miss!

Sunday, April 15, 2012

Shell Games Program at 2:00pm

Book Signing at 3:15pm

Muscatine History and Industry Center
117 West Second Street
Muscatine, Iowa 52761

Get your copy of Shell Games today! $21.95 at the Muscatine History and Industry Center.

Type 1: This is a sample of the type of postcard sent out to targeted individuals and groups to announce a book event—to help with promotion. Please examine it closely. Note that the specific time and location of the event are listed. A representative image is also included. The reverse of this particular postcard had space for a personal note of invitation. Note: This postcard sample is used courtesy of the Muscatine History and Industry Center in Muscatine, Iowa.

....

Type 2: For a postcard used to announce the publication of a book, the "front" of the postcard typically has the title of the book, a representative image, and the author's name. The reverse of the postcard would then include a short description of the book and any other information the author feels would be important to know. Please examine the sample above. Also, feel free to use it as a model for creating your own postcards.

Text for Reverse of Postcard:

John Fairfield was one of the most gifted and notorious abolitionist fighting for freedom for all in the decade before the American Civil War. In the pages of Finding Fairfield, *Jeffrey Copeland recounts his adventures in gathering the details and information needed to bring Fairfield's tale to life. These adventures took him to historic homes, important landmarks of the pre-Civil War era, Underground Railroad depots/museums, and other sites frequented by John Fairfield and others who proudly carried the torch of abolitionism.*

Jeffrey's journey was not always an easy one: getting terribly lost in the middle of nowhere while searching the Sandy & Beaver Canal system (a waterway once used to transport runaway slaves, by boat, to freedom), participating in a "ghost tour" near one of the most important Underground Railroad havens, and even spending the night in a haunted inn where John Fairfield himself once slept.

Finding Fairfield *also recounts Copeland's efforts to re-trace the journey made by John Fairfield when he once led nine slaves from Kentucky to their freedom in Canada.* Finding Fairfield *is both the story of a writer's craft and an engaging travelogue—a combination sure to please those who love American history and stories of "important Americans" who have had such profound impact on the world we live in today.*

Finding Fairfield *is now available through your favorite e-book retailers.*

Appendix H: Promotional Fliers and Posters

When authors find themselves in situations where fliers and posters must be designed to help promote an upcoming book event, a good rule of thumb is to have the following parts in each:

   a. An image of the book cover.
   b. A picture of the author.
   c. A short description of the book.
   d. Name of the bookstore/organization sponsoring the event.
   e. Time and location of the event.

samples of these follow (next page). Please study them carefully. Also, feel free to use them as models for those you will need to create from events.

Sample 1: Poster announcing book event: (Note: Poster image used courtesy of the Missouri History Museum, St. Louis, Missouri)

The secrets roll along with the Mississippi.....

Shell Games

The Life and Times of Pearl McGill,
Industrial Spy and Pioneer Labor Activist

Jeffrey S. Copeland

Pearl's story as a young woman in Muscatine in 1910 through 1912...
a story and program that you won't want to miss!

Sunday, April 15, 2012
Shell Games Program at 2:00pm
Book Signing at 3:15pm

 Muscatine History
and Industry Center
117 West Second Street • Muscatine, Iowa 52761
563-263-1052

Get your copy of Shell Games today! $21.95 at the Muscatine and History Center.

*Sample 2: Poster announcing book event: (Note: Poster image
used courtesy of the Muscatine History and Industry Center,*

the writers talk
reading series

JEFF COPELAND

discusses his new book
Ain't No Harm to Kill the Devill

Ain't No Harm to Kill the Devil

The Life and Legend of John Fairfield, Abolitionist for Hire

**WEDNESDAY
FEBRUARY 11
3:00 P.M.
BARTLETT 1017**

Jeffrey S. Copeland is a professor of English in the Department of Languages and Literatures at the University of Northern Iowa, where he teaches courses in literature and English Education. He has authored numerous books, including *Young Adult Literature: A Contemporary Reader, Inman's War: A Soldier's Story of Life in a Colored Battalion in WWII, Olivia's Story: The Conspiracy of Heroes Behind 'Shelley V. Kraemer,' Shell Games: The Life and Times of Pearl McGill, Industrial Spy and Pioneer Labor Activist*, and *Ain't No Harm to Kill the Devil: The Life and Legend of John Fairfield, Abolitionist for Hire.*

One of the most intriguing characters in American history was John Fairfield, an unconventional abolitionist who helped slaves to freedom in the decade before the Civil War. His exploits were cited by Harriet Tubman, Frederick Douglass, and Levi Coffin (the "President" of the Underground Railroad). Sometimes he posed as a land buyer for the railroad, a poultry dealer, a dentist, and even a slaver. One time he led nearly two dozen slaves to freedom by pretending to be an undertaker taking the body of a slave across the Ohio River to a slave cemetery on the other side! Fairfield was seen by some as a scoundrel, a con man, and a criminal. Others saw him as a religious man who believed that the evils of slavery needed to be wiped away at any cost. In the end, all agreed that Fairfield was successful!

Sponsored by
the Department of
Languages & Literatures

Sample 3: Flier announcing book event: (Note: Flier image used courtesy of Dr. Jeremy Schraffenberger, President, "The Writers Talk" Reading Series)

CONTRIBUTORS

A: Event coordinators/Booksellers

All of the event coordinators and bookstores listed below contributed to this book, most in multiple fashions. These event coordinators and bookstores should be considered invaluable resources for authors, for three very specific reasons. First, these are among the finest booksellers in the country and are, therefore, also wonderful venues for conducting book events. Second, the event coordinators at these stores are among the very best, and most experienced, of those working in that role—and have a wealth of knowledge authors can tap into when designing book events, readings, and promotions. Finally, most host a very large number of author events each year, so they are also good places to go to see how other authors do their presentations.

A Room of One's Own Bookstore
315 W. Gorham St.
Madison, WI 53703
www.roomofonesown.com
   *Event Coordinator: Gretchen Treu

Anderson's Bookshop
123 W. Jefferson Ave.
Naperville, IL 60540
www.andersonsbookshop.com
   *Event & Publicity Coordinators: Candy Purdom and Ginny Wehrli-Hemmeter

Annie Bloom's Books
7834 SW Capitol Way
Portland, OR 97219
www.annieblooms.com
  *Event Coordinator: Michael Keefe

Antigone Books
411 North 4th Avenue
Tucson, AZ 85705
www.antigonebooks.com
  *Event Coordinator: Debbie Cross

Barnes & Noble Booksellers, Fenton, Missouri
721 Gravois Road
Fenton, MO 63026
http://store-locator.barnesandnoble.com/store/2232
  *Event Coordinator: Deborah Horn

Barnes & Noble Booksellers, Waterloo, Iowa
1518 Flammang Drive
Waterloo, IA 50702
http://store-locator.barnesandnoble.com/store/2168
  *Event Coordinator: Steve Olsson

Boneshaker Books
2002 23rd Avenue South
Minneapolis, MN 55404
www.boneshakerbooks.com
  Event Coordinator: Anna Bongiovanni

Book Passage Bookstore
1 Ferry Bldg. - Marketplace #42
San Francisco, CA 94111
www.bookpassage.com
  *Author Services Liaison & Director, Path to Publishing
  Program: Sam Barry

Bookworks
4022 Rio Grande Blvd. NW
Albuquerque, NM 87107
www.bkwrks.com
  *Marketing & Event Coordinator: Amanda Sutton

Boulder Book Store
1107 Pearl Street
Boulder, CO 80302
http://boulderbookstore.indiebound.com
   *Marketing and Promotions Manager: Stephanie Schindhelm

Burke's Book Store
936 S. Cooper St.
Memphis, TN 38104
www.burkesbooks.com
   *Event Coordinator: Corey Mesler

Carmichael's Bookstore
2720 Frankfort Avenue
Louisville, KY 40206
www.carmichaelsbookstore.com
   *Event Coordinator: Jay Schwandt

City Lights Books
281 Columbus Avenue at Broadway
San Francisco, CA 94133
www.citylights.com
   *Event Coordinator: Peter Maravelis

E. Shaver, Bookseller
326 Bull Street
Savannah, GA 31401
www.eshaverbooks.com
   *Event Coordinator: Michelle Fleegel

Full Circle Bookstore
1900 NW Expressway
Oklahoma City, OK 73118
www.fullcirclebooks.com
   *Event Coordinator: Dana Meister

Green Apple Books
506 Clement Street
San Francisco, CA 94118
www.greenapplebooks.com
   *Event Coordinator: Ronnie Carrier

Horton's Books
410 Adams Square
Carrolton, GA 30117
www.hortonsbooks.com
  *Event Coordinator: Dorothy Pittman

Kepler's Books
1010 El Camino Real
Menlo Park, CA 94025
www.keplers.com
  *Event Coordinator: Pam Grange

Left Bank Books
399 North Euclid
St. Louis, MO 63108
www.left-bank.com
  *Event Coordinator: Kris Kleindienst

Malaprop's Bookstore
55 Haywood St.
Asheville, NC 28801
www.malaprops.com
  *Author Event Host: Cindy Norris

Moe's Books
2476 Telegraph Avenue
Berkeley, CA 94704
www.moesbooks.com
  *Event Coordinator: Owen Hill

Mysterious Galaxy Bookstore
5943 Balboa Ave. #100
San Diego, CA 92111
www.mystgalaxy.com
  *Event Coordinator/Publicity Manager: Maryelizabeth Hart

Powell's Books
2720 NW 29th Ave.
Portland, OR 97210
www.powells.com
  *Event Coordinator: Jeremy Garber

Quail Ridge Books
Ridgewood Shopping Center
3522 Wade Ave.
Raleigh, NC 27607
www.quailridgebooks.com
  *Event Coordinator: Rene Martin

Read Street Books
229 West Read Street
Baltimore, MD 21201
www.readonread.com
(410) 669-4103
  *Event coordinators: Christina Bittner and Lisette Howe

Schuler Books & Music
2660 28th St. SE
Grand Rapids, MI 49512
www.schulerbooks.com
  *Event Coordinator: Emily Stavrou Schaefer

Skylight Books
1818 N. Vermont Ave.
Los Angeles, CA 90027
www.skylightbooks.com
  *Event Manager: Mary Williams

Square Books
160 Courthouse Square
Oxford, MS 38655
www.squarebooks.com
  *Event Coordinator: Richard Howorth

STL Books
100 W. Jefferson Avenue
Kirkwood, MO 63122
www.stlbooks.com
  *Event Coordinator and Owner: Robin Theiss

Subterranean Books
6275 Delmar Blvd.
St. Louis, MO 63130
http://store.subbooks.com
  *Event Coordinator and Owner: Kelly von Plonski

The Book Cellar
4736 North Lincoln Ave.
Chicago, IL 60625
www.bookcellarink.com
  *Event Coordinator: Suzy Takas

The Book Lady Bookstore
6 East Liberty Street
Savannah, GA 31401
www.thebookladybookstore.com
  *Event Host: Christopher Blaker

The Next Chapter Bookstore
141 East Main St.
Northville, MI 48167
www.readnextchapterbooks.com
  *Event Coordinator: Annie Leonard

Watchung Booksellers
54 Fairfield Street
Montclair, NJ 07043
www.watchungbooksellers.com
  *Event Coordinator: Margot Sage-El

B: Authors

The following authors also shared their experience and expertise, on multiple levels, for this book. These outstanding writers also represent a wide range of the types of books in the
publishing world. Their author websites (or other contact
information) are also, if available, listed below. While most
of their websites have "common elements," all are worthy of
study to help new(er) authors discover how these sites are
used to reach out to readers and to promote her/his work and
book activities. Representative publications are also listed for
each author.

Arnold Adoff
Books include *Slow Dance Heartbreak Blues* and *Roots and Blues: A Celebration.*
www.arnoldadoff.com

Jimmy Santiago Baca
Books include *Stories from the Edge* and *A Glass of Water*
www.jimmysantiagobaca.com

Brod Bagert
Books include *Poetry for Young People: Edgar Allan Poe* and *School Fever*
www.brodbagert.com

T.C. Boyle
Books include *The Women: A Novel* and *T.C. Boyle Stories II: The Collected Stories of T. Coraghessan Boyle, Volume II*
www.tcboyle.com

Nancy White Carlstrom
Books include *This Is the Day!* and *Guess Who's Coming, Jesse Bear*
www.nancywhitecarlstrom.com

G. Scott Cawelti
Books include *The Complete Poetry of James Hearst* and *Brother's Blood: A Heartland Cain and Abel*
www.scottcawelti.com

Brad Cook
President, St. Louis Writers Guild
www.stlwritersguild.org

Jeffrey S. Copeland
Books include *Shell Games: The Life and Times of Pearl McGill, Industrial Spy and Pioneer Labor Activist* and *Ain't No Harm to Kill the Devil: The Life and Legacy of John Fairfield, Abolitionist for Hire*
http://jscottcopelandauthor.com

Chris Crowe
Books include *Two Roads* and *Getting Away with Murder: The True Story of the Emmett Till Case*
www.chriscrowe.com

Chris Crutcher
Books include *Period 8* and *Chinese Handcuffs*
www.chriscrutcher.com

Nikki Giovanni
Books include *Chasing Utopia: A Hybrid* and *Rosa*
www.nikki-giovanni.com

Mel Glenn
Books include *Foreign Exchange: A Mystery in Poems* and *The Taking of Room 114: A Hostage Drama in Poems*
www.melglenn.com

Jen Hasheider
President, Saturday Writers
www.saturdaywriters.org

Jane Henderson
Book Editor, *St. Louis Post-Dispatch*
www.stltoday.com

Mary Ann Hoberman
Books include *A House Is a House for Me* and *And to Think That We Thought That We'd Never Be Friends*
www.maryannhoberman.com

Wendy Marie Hoofnagle
Book Reviewer
Works include *Other Nations: The Hybridization of Medieval Insular Mythology and Identity* and *The Continuity of the Conquest: Charlemagne and Anglo-Norman Imperialism*
www.uni.edu/langlit/hoofnagle

Lee Bennett Hopkins
Books include *Lullaby and Kisses Sweet: Poems to Love with Your Baby* and *Incredible Inventions*
www.leebennetthopkins.com

Jerome Klinkowitz
Books include *Kurt Vonnegut's America* and *Frank Lloyd Wright and His Manner of Thought.*
Contact by postal mail only

Constance Levy
Books include *A Tree Place: And Other Poems* and *When Whales Exhale: and Other Poems*
www.constancelevy.com

J. Patrick Lewis
Books include *The House* and *Harlem Hellfighters*
www.jpatricklewis.com

Kevin O'Brien
Books include *Unspeakable* and *The Last Victim*
www.kevinobrienbooks.com

Jim O'Loughlin
President, Final Thursday Reading Series
Books include *The Late NIght Book* and *Daily Life in the Industrial United States,*
1870-1900.
www.jimoloughlin.com

Rob Rains
Books include *Intentional Walk: An Inside Look at the Faith that Drives the St. Louis Cardinals* and *James Naismith: The Man Who Invented Basketball*
Stlsportspage.com
Twitter = @RobRains

Delia Ray
Books include *Here Lies Linc* and *Ghost Girl: A Blue Ridge Mountain Story*
http://deliaray.com

Luis Rodriguez
Books include *Always Running: La Vida Loca: Gang Days in L.A.* and *It Calls You Back: An Odyssey through Love, Addiction, Revolutions, and Healing*
luisjrodriguez.com

Jeremy Schraffenberger
Associate Editor, *North American Review*
Works include *St. Joe's Passion* and "Kentucky News Butch."
www.northamericanreview.org

Gary Soto
Books include *Buried Onions* and *Baseball in April and Other Stories*
www.garysoto.com

Grant Tracey
Editor, *North American Review*
Books include *Playing Mac: A Novella in Two Acts, and Other Scenes* and *Parallel Lines and the Hockey Universe*
www.northamericanreview.org

Sally Walker
Books include *Boundaries: How the Mason-Dixon Line Settled a Family Feud and Divided a Nation* and *Secrets Of A Civil War Submarine: Solving The Mysteries Of The H. L. Hunley*
www.sallymwalker.com

Robert James Waller
Books include *The Bridges of Madison County* and *The Long Night of Winchell Dear: A Novel*
Contact by mail only

Acknowledgments

No book of this type would be complete without acknowledging those who provided the guidance, expertise, and "benefit of experiences" through the years. For me, these individuals would first include the many wonderful and talented bookstore events coordinators I've had the pleasure of working with across the globe when preparing for book events.

Special thanks should also be given to all of the authors who have shared with me their stories "from the road"—what worked for them and what went horribly awry at their events. I'm especially grateful for all the times my sides hurt from laughing while listening to their tales—and for the poignant stories of special times spent with their readers.

I'd like to thank the bookstore event coordinators and authors listed in the Contributors section of this book. So many of them helped shape me and put up with me as an author and presenter as my own "event presentation style" evolved.

There are several other organizations and individuals I'd like to make special note of here. I'd like to thank the Authors Guild (in my judgment the best organization of support and advocacy for writers ever), the National Council of Teachers of English (for the opportunity to hone my presentation skills through the years at their conferences), and independent booksellers everywhere (for providing such a wonderful array of venues for authors to showcase their works). I'd also like to thank my editor, Rosemary Yokoi, for believing in this project—and for her wonderful guidance and support.

I'd also like to offer special thanks to those who allowed use of photos and images for the book: Dr. Jeremy Schraffenberger, President, UNI's "The Writers Talk Reading Series," for permission to use the image of a flier for one of their events; the Missouri History Museum for permission to use the image of one of their posters; the Muscatine History and Industry Center for use of the image of one of their promotional postcards.

Finally, I'd like to single out three individuals in particular who have had the greatest influence upon my style of conducting book readings and events: Brod Bagert (for his incredible energy and modeling how to engage audiences), Arnold Adoff (for teaching me that grace and dignity can coexist with joyful mayhem during book events), and my wife, Linda (for sharing with me the universe of technology authors have at their fingertips while standing before audiences).

Thank you—and bless you all.

—JSC